The Big Book of Nature Projects

The Children's School of Science
original photography by Len Rubenstein

THAMES AND HUDSON

Contents

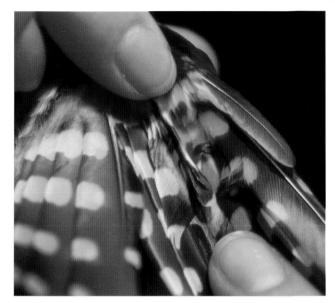

Explore the World of Birds

page 39

Adventures in Woods, Ponds & Fields

page 9

Living at the Seashore

page 59

Meet the Arthropods

page 105

Bugs, Bugs, Bugs

page 85

4

Copyright © 1997 Thames and Hudson Inc.
First published in the United States of America in 1997 by Thames and Hudson Inc.,
500 Fifth Avenue, New York, New York 10110

Photos copyright © Len Rubenstein unless otherwise indicated.

Library of Congress Catalog Card Number 96-61458
ISBN 0–500–01773–5

Cover design by Liz Trovato
Interior design and typesetting by BTD
Color separations by The Sarabande Press
Managing Editor: Laurance Rosenzweig

Printed and Bound in Hong Kong

Introduction

The kids you see in this book had a great time exploring the natural world, and you will too!

In your backyard and basement, at the park down the street, and at your local beach or pond, plants and animals are growing and changing all the time, sometimes in astounding ways. People who explore this amazing world are called naturalists, and this book will show you how to be a naturalist yourself.

One thing naturalists do is go out to observe plants and animals in their natural settings. Sometimes they collect specimens to study more closely. This book will show you how to make your own field trips to observe and collect plant and animal specimens. Among many other things, you'll:

• Identify different kinds of birds by their plumage, their outlines, their
  unique songs, and the different sorts of nests they build
• Set up a transect line at the seashore with string and two sticks, and then
  use it to do a species survey of all the animals along the line
• Explore a pond with an underwater viewer and collect flatworms, mud
  snails, and microscopic invertebrates
• Cut and press wildflowers, ferns, and other wild plants.

We'll also show you how to make different kinds of temporary environments for some of the plants and animals you collect, so you can keep observing them for days or weeks at home.

As you start asking yourself why animals do all the unusual things they do, you can look for the answers yourself with the projects and experiments in this book. You'll be able to:

• Discover why chickens turn their eggs by hatching your own eggs in an incubator
• Watch how crayfish defend their territory from other crayfish in a pan of water
• See what predatory birds eat by taking apart an owl pellet
• Understand the process of insect metamorphosis by watching a caterpillar
  turn itself into a monarch butterfly.

You'll also learn how to use the tools that naturalists use, like butterfly nets, microscopes, plant presses, Berlese funnels, and bird nest viewers— you can even build some of them yourself!

No matter where you live, in the city or the country, there is plenty of nature around you if you look for it. If you can't find the right plant or animal for one of your projects, you can order everything from live sponges to earthworms and crickets through the mail, using the information on page 124. And if you come across a word you don't understand, just look it up in the Glossary on page 126.

Safety Tips

The field trips and outdoor projects in this book will show you how to observe and collect plants and animals in woods, fields, ponds, and at the shore. If you follow a few simple rules, your adventures will be safe and enjoyable:

• Plan your outings with your parents or guardians, even if you are going to a familiar place. Make sure that they know if you plan to go into even shallow water.
• Wear the right clothes. Protect your feet when wading; protect your arms and legs in heavy underbrush.
• Always take a friend with you.

Classification

o one really knows how many animals live on this planet. Well over a million different kinds, or **species**, have been described and named already. Scientists think there might be a million or two more that exist, but just haven't been discovered yet.

Millions of animals

It's hard to imagine one or two million different animals! How can we make sense of such diversity? One way is to categorize animals, or put them into groups, instead of thinking of an endless list of individual species. People often invent categories that express the important similarities and differences we see among animals. For instance, we speak of **domestic animals**—pets, livestock, and other animals we breed and raise—and **wild animals**—those that breed and find food without our intervention. And we speak of **pests**—those creatures that eat our food crops or damage our property—and **beneficial animals**—those that eat our pests or provide us with food or materials. Scientists have devised systems of classification that attempt to reflect what they understand about the evolutionary history of different animals, as well as their anatomy, physiology, and ecology.

Taxonomy

Scientists have divided up the million or so known animals into about twenty-six groups. (Scientists don't all agree about this division; some combine or further divide groups.) These groups are called **phyla**. Phyla are broad collections of animals that have important things in common, but may be quite different from one another in appearance and habit. For example, we belong to the

phylum Chordata, as do guinea pigs, hummingbirds, herring, bullfrogs, sea squirts, lancelets, and lampreys. Tarantulas, butterflies, horseshoe crabs, shrimp, and pillbugs all share the phylum Arthropoda.

Phyla are divided into **classes**, classes into **orders**, orders into **families**, and families into **genera**. Each time a division is made,

the animals that are most closely related are grouped together. Finally, animals are sorted into distinct species. Members of a species can reproduce to create more animals like themselves.

Scientists who are primarily interested in the classification of the animals they study are called **taxonomists**.

Phylum Chordata

Phylum Arthropoda

Naming animals

Many animals have more than one name, and many share a name with other species. "Grasshopper" and "locust" both name the same animal. Grasshopper and locust also name dozens of other, similar looking animals! To avoid confusion, scientists use a two-part Latin name to label each species. *Dissosteira carolina* names the Carolina grasshopper; the first part of the name is shared by all the related species that make up one genus, while the second part is given to just one species. Both common and scientific names will be used throughout this book.

Some invertebrates look so much alike that it takes an expert to identify each to the level of species. Often, you will be satisfied to simply know what phylum or class a particular animal belongs to. Taxonomy boxes will list this information for most of the animals pictured in this book.

Taxonomy

PHYLUM:
  Arthropoda (animals with paired, jointed legs and a hard exoskeleton)
CLASS: Insecta (the insects)
ORDER: Orthoptera (crickets, grasshoppers, praying mantids, and their relatives)
GENUS: Dissosteira
SPECIES: Dissosteira carolina (carolina grasshopper)

8

Adventures in Woods, Ponds and Fields

Some scientists are interested in the relationships between different kinds of plants and animals, as well as the connections between these living things and the non-living things around them. They wonder how certain plants and animals survive in particular places. They think about how one change, such as an increase in temperature or rainfall, might cause other changes. They examine ways that creatures depend on one another, and ways they compete. These scientists are ecologists.

The word ecology comes from the Greek word for house. You can think of ecology as the study of plants and animals at home, in their natural environment. This chapter focuses on three common and very different environments: woods, which are cool and shady; ponds, which are wet, muddy, and usually sunny; and fields, which are dry, sunny, and warm. Each has its own kinds of plants and animals, and its own ecological patterns.

This chapter has projects designed for each of these environments. When you're in the woods, you'll learn how to perform a survey of the many invertebrate animals living in a patch of soil (p. 18), and how to make ink prints from the leaves you find (p. 12). You'll also use a Berlese funnel to find small animals in the soil of woody areas, including earthworms which you can take home and study as well (pp. 20 and 14). In fields and meadow areas, you'll be able to collect and press wildflowers (p. 26); you'll also find crickets and grasshoppers that you can bring home and study in a terrarium (p. 24). And at your local pond, you'll be able to look for fish and other freshwater animals with a wood-and-Plexiglas underwater viewer that you can build for yourself (p. 32). You'll also study the amazing regeneration abilities of flatworms (p. 36) and the hidden world of aquatic microinvertebrates (p. 30), both of which live in ponds.

Almost everything in this section can be made or collected, but you can also order the animals and equipment from the supply houses on page 124.

The Woods

Woods are places where lots of trees grow. Shady and cool, they are special places to explore.Some woods are filled with evergreen **conifers**, like pines, firs, and hemlocks. Others have broad-leaved **deciduous** trees, like oaks and maples, that lose their leaves in autumn. Many woodlands have both kinds of trees. What are the woods like where you live?

Telling trees apart

Most woodlands contain many different kinds of plants. Ferns, mosses, and tiny wildflowers carpet the ground, and various shrubs and saplings stand over them. Then, of course, there are the trees. Each kind, or **species**, has characteristics that will help you tell it apart from others. Choose a tree to study, and look carefully at the shape of its leaves, and the color and texture of the bark. Then look to see if you can find other trees like it nearby.

Maple trees have broad leaves with several large parts, or lobes. Elms have oblong leaves with many small "teeth" along the edges.

Often, a few species of trees dominate a woodland; that is, they outnumber other species, and take up the most space. Ecologists describe woodlands according to their dominant trees. For example, you may live near an oak-pine forest, a spruce forest, a beech-maple forest, or a redwood forest.

Most oak trees can be put into one of two groups. Those in the white oak group have leaves with rounded lobes, and acorns that ripen within one year. Trees in the black oak group have leaves with pointed lobes, and acorns that take two years to mature.

You can make leaf or bark rubbings to help you remember the different trees you find. Sketches that show the basic shape of a tree, or details like flowers or buds, are also helpful. A field guide to the trees will help you name the trees you have learned to recognize.

A young green heron perches in oak tree.

Making Leaf Prints

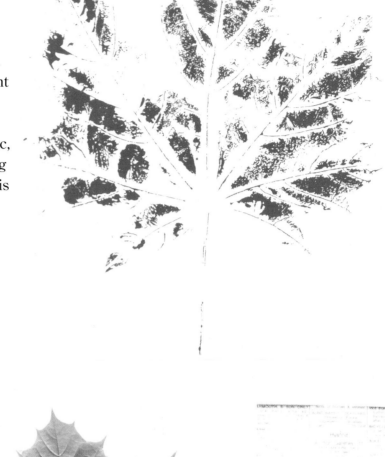

 You can use leaf prints to record the shape and pattern of veins you notice in different kinds of leaves, or to create beautiful designs on paper, T-shirts, or other surfaces. If you are printing on fabric, make sure to use acrylic paint or a printing ink that will not wash out when the fabric is laundered. Experiment with different leaves, inks, and printing surfaces to see what effects you like best.

Materials:

- newspaper
- acrylic paint or water-base printing ink*
- tray, or pane of glass with taped edges
- brayer (the ink roller)*
- leaves
- paper or cloth

* ACRYLIC PAINT, INK, AND BRAYERS ARE AVAILABLE AT ART SUPPLY STORES. IF YOU ARE PRINTING ON FABRIC, MAKE SURE TO USE ACRYLIC PAINT OR A PRINTING INK THAT WILL NOT WASH OUT WHEN THE FABRIC IS WASHED.

Directions:

1. Cover your work space with a layer of old newspaper.

2. Squeeze a small amount of ink onto the tray or glass.

3. Roll the brayer in the ink to coat it.

4. Place a leaf on a sheet of newspaper. Use the brayer to coat the leaf with ink. If you coat the underside of the leaf, the veins will print more clearly.

5. Press down on the leaf with your fingers. Try to press each part of it. Put the leaf, ink side down, on a piece of paper or fabric.

6. Remove the leaf by slowly pulling the stem and edges straight up off the paper or cloth.

Earthworms

I f you conduct a soil survey in a yard, garden, or woods, you'll probably uncover earthworms. These burrowing animals tunnel through the ground by pushing their "heads" through the soil and swallowing it in mouthfuls as they go. Swallowed soil is excreted and pressed against the walls of the tunnel, or carried up to the surface and deposited as **castings**.

Earthworms belong to the phylum Annelida. All annelids have segmented bodies that look as if they are made of many small sections.

ALL PHOTOS ON THIS SPREAD © ASSOCIATES OF CAPE COD

What about them?

Earthworms have no eyes, but special light-sensitive cells in their skin allow them to tell light from dark. They usually avoid strong light, burrowing in the ground during the daytime and coming out to feed or mate at night. Earthworms are **hermaphrodites**; individuals have both male and female reproductive organs. When they mate, two pair up on the ground with their bodies alongside one another. Each transfers sperm to the other. A few

days later, each worm's "collar," or **clitellum**, starts to make a cocoon for the eggs. It slips like a band over the worm's body, picking up eggs and sperm as it does. Eventually, the cocoon slips right off the worm and into the soil. The tiny eggs within it hatch within a few weeks.

Raising earthworms

Housing: You can raise earthworms in a dishpan, picnic cooler, or gallon glass jar. Fill your container with loose, moist soil. Use soil that is high in organic matter rather than sand or clay. Try to gather soil from the spot where you collect your worms so you know that it will suit them. Keep the container away from direct sunlight, and mist the soil with water if it starts to dry out. Make a cardboard cover with holes for ventilation. A one gallon jar will house ten or twelve worms. Larger containers can hold many more.

Food: Earthworms eat fresh and decaying plants they find around their burrows, and organic matter found in the soil. Feed your worms every other week by sprinkling moist cornmeal or bread crumbs on top of the soil. You can also add a few leaves to the container. Remove uneaten food before it rots.

Habits: If you want to observe mating or feeding, you'll probably need to make observations at night. During the day, you can unearth a few worms and place them on damp paper toweling in order to get a closer look at them.

Buying worms: If you aren't able to collect worms outdoors, you can order them from one of the suppliers on page 124, or buy "nightcrawlers" sold for fish bait.

An earthworm experiment
Collect:
- two or three live, healthy earthworms
- a large, clean glass jar
- several soil samples of different colors (collect them from different depths or places)
- fresh leaves
- waxed paper
- a rubber band
- a paper bag or aluminum foil

Procedure:
- Layer the different soil samples in the jar. Mist the soil slightly if it is extremely dry. Put fresh leaves on top of the soil and add the worms.
- Punch small holes in the waxed paper. Fasten it over the opening of the jar with a rubber band.

- Carefully observe the jar and record what you see.
- Place the jar in the paper bag and staple the bag shut. Keep it at room temperature for two weeks.

- Every few days remove the jar and study it carefully. How have the earthworms affected the soil?

Taxonomy

PHYLUM: *Annelida (the segmented worms)*
CLASS: *Oligochaeta (3100 species, including earthworms)*
ORDER: *Haplotaxida*
SUBORDER: *Lumbricina (includes three orders of earthworms)*
FAMILY: *Lumbricidae*
GENUS: *Lumbricus, Eisenia, and others (earthworms)*
SPECIES: *Lumbricus terrestris, and other species*

Snails

Snails belong to a group of soft-bodied animals that make up the phylum Mollusca. Many molluscs have shells. These shells are secreted by the mantle, a special body part unique to molluscs.

Land snails

Once in a while, a land snail shows up at the grocery store, accidentally shipped in with a load of produce. More often, you'll find them crawling around in the damp leaves on a forest floor, in gardens, or hiding out from the hot sun underneath a rock.

Land snails have four movable feelers, or **tentacles,** at the front end of their bodies. All of these are sensitive to touch, and the longer two have eyes at their tips. Land snails can tell light from dark, but their eyes don't form images.

How do snails move?

Snails are in the class Gastropoda, which means "stomach foot." A large, muscular foot runs the length of a snail's body. When the muscles in this foot contract, the snail glides along. Tiny hair-like **cilia** cover the bottom of the foot, and their movements also propel the snail. The foot, like the rest of the snail's body, is covered with slimy mucus.

The mucus lubricates, or greases, the surface the snail is on, helping it glide more easily. Watch a snail move along your arm or on the ground. You may see the shiny trail of mucus it leaves behind.

Eating

Most land and water snails have a special structure in their mouths called a **radula.** The radula is kind of like a tongue covered with rows of tiny teeth. A snail can use it to scrape away on food, filing off tiny bits and pulling them into its mouth. Some land snails have specialized diets, while others eat many different things. Many snails are **herbivores,** feeding on fruits, vegetables, leaves, and fungi. Some are **carnivores,** and eat worms and other snails.

Rearing land snails

You can keep one or two land snails in a gallon glass jar with paper toweling or coffee filters on the bottom. Use only white paper, as some inks and dyes may be harmful to snails. A terrarium may seem like a more natural environment, but it's much harder to keep clean and mold-free. Make sure the jar has a lid so your snails don't escape. Wire screening or cheesecloth will let air in.

Remove the old paper and scrub the jar clean at least once a week. Thoroughly dampen fresh paper with water and layer it on the bottom. Moist paper will be easier for the snails to crawl on, and it will humidify the air. Humidity is

important. If the air and paper get too dry, your snails will **aestivate**, or pull their bodies into their shells and stick themselves to the side of the jar with mucus. This allows them to withstand unfavorable conditions, but it won't allow you to observe feeding and other interesting behavior. If the air is always very humid, or you don't clean the jar often enough, mold or bacteria might grow and kill the snails.

When you clean the jar, clean the snails off, too. Just rinse them in cool tap water. They are apt to come out of their shells and crawl around after their "shower," making this a fun time to hold and watch them.

Captive land snails will eat the damp paper you line the jar with,

so they are easy to feed. You can also give them a bit of lettuce, carrot, or apple on occasion. Make sure to remove leftovers and clean the jar after offering fresh food so that mold and bacteria don't grow. A small piece of oyster shell in the jar will provide the snail with a source

of calcium, a mineral needed for shell growth.

If you have to go away for a few weeks, your snails will probably not need any special care. Clean their jar before you leave, and add fresh, damp paper but no other food. As the paper dries out, the snails will aestivate. They can remain in this condition for a month or longer as long as the jar does not become moldy, freezing cold, or overheated. Keep the jar out of direct sunlight so the snails won't get overheated and die.

Taxonomy

PHYLUM: **Mollusca (soft-bodied marine animals)**

CLASS: **Gastropoda (snails, slugs, and limpets)**

SUBCLASS: **Pulmonata (slugs and most land snails. Mantle cavity has become a lung. Hermaphroditic.)**

ORDER: **Stylommatophora (two pairs of tentacles, with eyes on top of the second pair)**

17

INVERTEBRATES

Start your search for invertebrates by looking on the ground. A yard or park is a good place to look. So is the edge of a pathway or sidewalk. You'll find insects, worms, and many other familiar invertebrate animals in these places.

Attracting invertebrates

Some animals are comfortable in dry air and bright sunshine. Others prefer cool, moist, shady places. Experiment to see what conditions attract different invertebrates by placing an old board or wooden shingle on the ground. You might want to label it so passersby know to leave it where they find it.

Check each day to see if any animals are under your shingle. Compare what you find under the shingle to what you find next to it.

Digging deeper

Japanese beetle larvae, earthworms, and centipedes are all invertebrates that spend a substantial amount of time underground. Avoiding fresh air and sunshine, they go about their business under our feet. Sometimes we get clues about life underground. Holes at the surface may lead to burrows and nests below. Soil-dwellers may search for food aboveground at night or early in the morning. Other times we have to search to discover what lives under us.

UNDERFOOT

Conducting a soil-animal survey

A survey is a detailed study. To find out what sort of animals live underground, begin by surveying a small area. You can work on dry land, or in the wet sediment along a pond shore or marsh. First, mark off a square plot measuring anywhere from six inches to one yard on a side. Then, gently remove the upper few inches of soil with a garden trowel and sift through it with your fingers. Keep a record of any animals you find. What do they look like? How deep in the soil did you find them? How many of each kind were present?

Continue to remove and search through layers of soil until you've dug as deep as you wish. Carefully replace both soil and animals when you are through.

Using a Berlese Funnel

A Berlese funnel (also called a Tullgren funnel) can help you find out what animals live in leaf litter and soil. It will help you collect very tiny animals that you might otherwise overlook. You can make your own Berlese funnel from equipment you buy or find around the house, or you can order a funnel from one of the companies listed on page 124.

Materials

- a large plastic or metal funnel
- glass vial, just big enough to fit over the narrow end of the funnel (optional)
- piece of coarse wire screen (a 1 centimeter or 1/4 inch mesh will do)
- wire cutters or tin snips
- jar, bucket, or three-legged stand to hold funnel
- some leaf litter or soil, freshly collected
- a gooseneck lamp, or an adjustable desk lamp
- jar lid or petri dish

Directions

1. Cut a circular piece from the wire screen with the wire cutters or tin snips. Make the circle three or more inches in diameter.
2. If you are using a purchased funnel that comes with a glass collecting vial, slip the vial onto the small end of the funnel.

3. Place the circular screen inside the funnel.

4. Set the funnel on the three-legged stand, or place it in a jar or bucket that will hold the funnel upright.

5. Fill the funnel several inches deep with leaf litter. Make sure to use fresh litter that you've collected that day.

6. Turn on the lamp, and position it so that the bulb shines down onto the leaf litter. Make sure the bulb is close enough to warm the litter, but not positioned in a way that might melt a plastic funnel!

7. After half an hour or so, lift the funnel and look into the collecting vial, bucket, or jar. If no animals are present, set the funnel back under the light and wait a while longer. You may want to check your funnel frequently at first to see how long it takes for animals to begin dropping into the jar. You can leave your funnel under the light for as long as you want, provided you are nearby.

8. Study the creatures you have collected. You might want to put some in a jar lid or plastic petri dish so that you can observe them with a hand lens or microscope. You will probably find animals that are new to you, as well as some familiar ones.

9. When you are through, return the animals you collected to the litter or soil they crawled out of. Put the litter or soil back where you found it.

Real Pseudo

You may find a pseudoscorpion among the animals you collect with your Berlese funnel. Although pseudoscorpions are common in leaf litter, they are so small that people usually don't notice them. Most pseudoscorpions are less than two-tenths of an inch long. Though they do have fierce-looking pincers, they are too small to pinch or bite a person. They prey on tiny insects.

Note: You can use a mothball instead of a light bulb to drive the animals out of the litter. Simply tape a mothball to a piece of wood or cardboard large enough to cover the open top of your funnel. Place the board on the funnel, with the mothball "inside," over the litter. Use the funnel outdoors, on the porch, or in another well-ventilated area, since it isn't healthy to inhale mothball fumes.

Fields

 Fields are open stretches of land where crops, grasses, or wildflowers grow.

The plants that grow in a field get lots of sun. Some fields occur naturally. Others are created when people clear trees from land in order to build or plant crops.

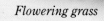
Flowering grass

What are flowers?

We appreciate flowers for their beauty, but they are not merely decorative. Flowers contain special organs that can produce seeds, the means by which many plants reproduce. Not all plants have flowers, but lots of familiar ones do. Some are large and showy. Others, like the flowers on certain trees and grasses, are often overlooked.

Black-eyed Susans (above) are common in fields and along roadsides in the midwestern and eastern United States. The dark brown center of each "flower" is actually a cluster of many tiny flowers.

Changes

A field may have dozens of different wildflowers in bloom at once. You may notice that a few seem to dominate the landscape, while others are few in number, or hidden underneath larger, bolder, blossoms. Which flowers are common in the fields near your home?

Each kind of flower blooms at a particular time. Dandelions bloom in spring and early summer, while goldenrod flowers from late summer to fall. As you get familiar with a field, you will start to notice that when one type of flower wilts, another comes into bloom. Keep track of the patterns you notice. You may see connections between the lives of the birds and insects you observe in a field, and the flowers you have been watching. The American goldfinch, for example, has an unusually late nesting season, from July through September. Sunflowers, thistles, and many other wildflowers have developed seeds by late summer, providing a good supply of food for the adult goldfinches and their growing young.

SUMMER SINGERS

In late summer and early fall, fields are filled with the rhythmic chirping and trilling of thousands of insects. Sit quietly and listen. How many different sounds can you hear? Listen at different times during the day and night. Insects that are quiet at one time may be noisy at another.

Grasshopper Nymph

Who's making all that noise?

Some of the most familiar field sounds are the mating calls made by grasshoppers and crickets. Usually, it's the males who sing, but in some species males and females call to each other. Grasshoppers make sounds by rubbing their hind legs against their wings, while crickets rub a ridge on one wing across a scraper on the other. There are many species of grasshoppers and crickets, and each has a different call. Even when you can't spot the singer, you may recognize its song.

Female Cricket

Finding grasshoppers and field crickets

You may notice grasshoppers chewing on plant stems, or they may surprise you as they jump or fly out of your way. Look for crickets on the ground, under litter or stones, and in piles of grass clippings, hay, or weeds.

In warm climates you can find these insects throughout the year. In cooler climates, where autumn frosts kill the adults, they overwinter as eggs in the ground. In the spring, the young, called nymphs, emerge from the eggs. By mid-summer many nymphs have matured, and adults are again plentiful. If you can, catch a few nymphs or adults. They are easy to raise, and interesting to watch.

If you're quick, you may be able to catch a grasshopper with your bare hands.

Raising grasshoppers and field crickets

Food: Crickets can eat an enormous variety of things: plants, other insects, even cloth and leather! Dry dog food pellets are another food possibility for captive crickets. You can vary their diet with small slices of fruit and vegetables. Give grasshoppers fresh leaves from grasses and other field plants, or green vegetables. Make sure you remove old food before it starts to rot.

Numbers: Crickets and grasshoppers need plenty of space. Too many in one container may cause them to be aggressive and injure one another. Male crickets often claim a particular territory, make sounds to warn others away, and chase or kick intruders. If your container is small (a one-gallon fish tank, for example) keep only one male and a female or two. Larger containers, well supplied with hiding places and things to crawl on, can hold more.

Behavior to look for

What do crickets and grasshoppers do? Watch carefully to see. You may notice
- eating
- drinking
- grooming
- chirping
- responses to chirping
- mating
- egg laying

Compare the observations you make indoors to those you make in the field. It is much easier to observe a grasshopper or cricket over time when you bring it indoors, but captive animals do not always behave just as they would in the wild.

Housing: Keep grasshoppers and crickets in glass or clear plastic containers. Add a tight-fitting top made from wire screening or cheesecloth. Layer an inch or two of sand, soil, or peat moss on the bottom of the container so that females will have a place to lay their eggs. Sterilize the soil by baking it at 200 degrees for two hours, so bacteria and fungi will be slower to grow. Mist the soil with water, and check it periodically. Some moisture will encourage females to lay eggs, and it may help the eggs develop, but they won't hatch if the soil is really wet. Add a few stones, cardboard tubes, or other "hiding places."

Water: A clean piece of sponge plugged into a small bottle of water will provide a continuing supply of water. A jar lid containing a wet piece of sponge, or a few drops of water sprinkled on rocks or food will work as well.

Collecting and

Botanists, the scientists who study plants, sometimes collect leaves and flowers to press. The pressed specimens are a useful record of the different species that grow in a particular area.

Field notes

Take note of details that will help you remember and identify the plants you collect. How big was the plant? Where was it growing? What color were the flowers and leaves? Pressed specimens look faded and flat compared to freshly collected ones, so good notes and sketches are important!

Making a herbarium

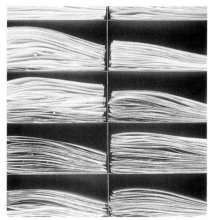

Pressing dries and preserves plant specimens. Mounted, identified, and labeled, a collection of pressed specimens makes up a **herbarium**. Herbariums are useful to researchers and students who want to learn more about different kinds of plants. You can make your own herbarium. First, make yourself a plant press.

Collecting plants

You can use a scissors or pocket knife to cut your own specimens. If you are collecting grasses or wildflowers, cut a long enough piece of stem to get both blossoms and leaves. Some flowers can be collected throughout the day, but others must be cut early because they wilt or close up in the afternoon.

Find out if any plants in your area are rare and should not be collected. Check with a local nature center, or consult a list of protected species to find out. Also make sure you recognize poison ivy and other irritating plants that are best left alone!

Pressing Plants

You'll need:

- Newspaper.
- Five or ten pieces of corrugated cardboard, 8"x10" or larger.*
- White construction paper or blotter paper.
- Two pieces of Masonite, very stiff cardboard, or end boards made of wooden slats. These should be the same size as the corrugated cardboard, or slightly larger.
- Two straps with buckles, or with Velcro sewn on as a fastener.
- * A plant press can be any size you find useful. Try making a large one to keep at home, and a pocket size one to carry with you.

Place the end boards on the top and bottom of your layers of cardboard and paper.

Directions:

1. Put a few layers of newspaper on top of a piece of corrugated cardboard. Add two sheets of white paper and another layer of newspaper.
2. Repeat these steps, beginning with a new piece of cardboard, until you have only one piece of cardboard left.
3. Top off your stack with a final layer of cardboard, then sandwich the entire stack between the two pieces of Masonite, stiff cardboard, or end boards.
4. Use the straps to fasten the whole package together. Your plant press is ready to use!

Pressing your specimens

Open your plant press, and arrange your specimens between the pieces of white construction paper or blotting paper. Take care to keep plants from overlapping one another, or they will stick together and tear when you try to separate them. When all your specimens are positioned, fasten the straps of the press tightly. In a week or two you may open the press and remove the dry specimens.

A stack of books is a good substitute for straps.

Mounting pressed plants

Dried specimens can be glued or taped to heavy paper, or mounted under a layer of clear, adhesive-backed plastic. Botanists usually record the scientific name of each specimen in a herbarium, and group each plant with closely related species. Record the name of each plant you are able to identify on the paper that you mounted it on. Keep your collection in a notebook or folder.

PONDS

Ponds are wet places with mucky bottoms. Some are full of water all year round; others dry up in the summer. Ponds are usually shallow enough for sunlight to reach all the way to the bottom. Ponds form in different ways. Some were formed as glaciers retreated during the last ice age, some are carved by streams and rivers, and some are made by people or other animals. Many fascinating plants and animals live in, on, and around ponds. Some simple equipment will help you to find and study them.

Things to bring

- Old sneakers or rubber boots will protect your feet from sharp stones and broken glass.
- An aquatic net or kitchen strainer is useful for scooping samples from the pond bottom.
- A plastic hand lens will give you a close-up view of the smaller plants or animals you find.
- Binoculars are great for watching birds and turtles.
- A shallow pan or plastic bucket makes a good temporary aquarium for any small aquatic animals that you want to observe awhile before releasing.
- White enamel refrigerator pans, or light-colored plastic dishpans will make your catch easy to see.

Remember to plan your pond trips with an adult so you will know where you can explore safely, and bring along a friend.
Collect pond animals from the shore or by wading in shallow water.

Changes

Pond water may turn green with algae in the summer, and freeze solid in winter. Animals that are common during one season may be difficult to find in another. Visit a pond at different times of the year to learn about these changes.

28

Microinvertebrates

 Some invertebrates are so small that you need a hand lens or microscope to see them. Viewed closely enough, tree bark, pond scum, drying mud, and human skin reveal hidden layers of life on earth. Exploring the tiny worlds that exist within the one we know is fascinating. Look carefully; you'll find that tiny invertebrates are everywhere!

Collecting for the microscope

There are countless places to look for microinvertebrates. Think small!

You can begin your exploration of the unseen with a pond study. Stagnant, green water, mud from along the shore, and the slimy coating on rocks and aquatic plants are all worth collecting. Plastic containers can be used to dig up mud, floating algae, and duckweed. Leaves and stems of rooted aquatic plants can also be collected. You can simply scoop up water in a jar, or drag a fine mesh plankton net through the water to concentrate your sample.

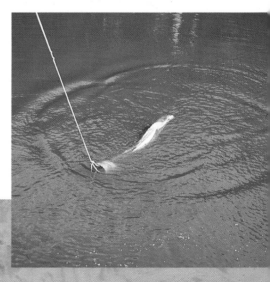

Observing your samples

Back home, get your samples ready to observe. Mud can be scraped into a plastic or enamel pan, and a little water poured over it. Aquatic plants can also be floated in pans of water. Jars containing water samples can be allowed to settle; leave the lids open a bit to allow fresh air to circulate.

Examine your samples with a hand lens to find tiny insect larvae, crustaceans, and molluscs that you might not have noticed when you were collecting. You may also find their eggs attached to plants, or floating in the water. A tiny leaf, drop of water, or bit of "slime" can be put on a glass slide under a compound microscope for an even closer look. Many of the animals you find may be unfamiliar and difficult to identify at first. Make drawings of the creatures you discover to help you recognize them when you see them again.

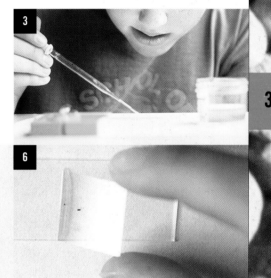

Buying magnifying equipment

There are many kinds of magnifiers. The cheapest and simplest to use is a hand lens. High quality plastic or glass hand lenses are available. Depending on the lens, these tools will allow you to magnify a specimen anywhere from three to ten times.

Another inexpensive and easy-to-use tool is the pocket microscope. Some have a battery-powered light, and can magnify as much as thirty times. Pocket microscopes are small and sturdy, so you can use them in the field as well as indoors. They cost between six and twenty dollars.

Compound microscopes are useful if you want to see very tiny animals. Specimens must be small enough to fit on a glass microscope slide, and thin enough for light to pass through them. Compound microscopes can magnify hundreds (sometimes even thousands) of times, making it possible to see things as small as individual cells. Compound microscopes vary widely in price. Sometimes high school and university science departments sell good, used microscopes for low prices when they are upgrading their equipment.

Dissecting microscopes, also called stereo microscopes, allow you to magnify large or opaque objects. They are great for examining pond animals, tree bark, insects, and soil.

Because they have two eyepieces, these microscopes provide good depth of field, making it possible to get quite a bit of an object in focus at once. Unfortunately, even inexpensive dissecting scopes are several hundred dollars. Check to see if a local school or science center has one you can use.

Looking Under Water

An underwater viewer,such as swim goggles or a diving mask,can help you see what is going on in a pond. It's easy to make your own viewer.

Making a coffee can viewer

A coffee can viewer is the easiest kind to make.

You will need:

- an extra-large juice can or coffee can
- a can opener
- heavy-duty plastic wrap
- duct tape

Instructions:

1. Use the can opener to remove both ends from the can.

One of the animals you can spot with your viewer is a mud snail.

2. Stretch a piece of heavy-duty plastic wrap across one opening.

3. Fasten the plastic wrap securely with duct tape, and you're done!

Take your viewer to a nearby pond, and lower the end with plastic wrap on it into the water. Peer into the open end to see what is below the surface.

A wood and plexiglass viewer

You can make a larger and more durable viewer out of wood and plexiglass.

You will need:

- four wooden boards, 8"x12" or larger
- wood screws
- wood glue
- washers for the screws
- a drill and a screwdriver
- a piece of plexiglass (sized to fit with your boards)
- non-toxic caulk (available at hardware stores)

Instructions:

1. Screw the four boards together to form the sides of a box. Make sure you put glue on the joints first.
2. Fit the plexiglass over the opening at one end, and fasten it in place with screws. Make sure to pre-drill holes in the plexiglass, so it won't crack when you put the screws in place. And use washers between the screwheads and the plexiglass to keep the holes from leaking.
3. Caulk all the joints with non-toxic caulk. Remember to caulk the plexiglass joints as well. When the caulk is dry, your viewer is ready to use.

Experiment with your finished viewer to figure out how to get a clear look at the pond bottom. You may have to put your face down into the box or can to block out reflections.

PLANARIA

Planaria belong to a large group of animals called the flatworms, or Platyhelminthes. Unlike annelid worms, their bodies are not segmented. Most flatworms are quite small. Many are parasites and live within the bodies of other animals, however, planaria are free-living. Planaria have smooth, flat bodies, and most species have just two eyes, though some have more. Their eyes simply tell light from dark, unlike ours which can form images and focus on near or far away objects. Most planaria avoid light, so scientists say they are **photonegative**.

Finding planaria

You can find planaria in streams, lakes, ponds, and other freshwater habitats. They are quite common, but you have to look closely to find them. Most are less than thirty millimeters long, and because they avoid light, they often spend the day under rocks or in decaying plants and bottom "muck." One good way to find planaria is to pick up a submerged stick or rock and turn it over. You may spot snails and leeches clinging to the surface, and tiny, brown or grey planaria gliding across. Even though they are small, the triangular heads and eyespots of planaria make them recognizable.

You can "fish" for planaria by tying a small piece of liver or other raw meat to a string and tossing it into the water. Half an hour later, pull the meat back up. Planaria that have come to feed on the meat will be pulled up along with it. This works better in running water than it does in stagnant water. Planaria get oxygen by absorbing it through their skin, or **epidermis**. In places where the water is stagnant and low in oxygen, you may have trouble finding them.

Planaria have been carefully studied in the laboratory, but scientists still have a lot to learn about the range and habits of different species in the wild.

Feeding

Planaria have mouths near the middle of their bodies, on the **ventral** (under) side. To eat, they stick a long tube called the **pharynx** out of their mouths. The pharynx works like a straw, sucking small particles and liquids into the stomach. Some planaria are particular about what they eat, and eject any unsuitable particles they ingest right back out through the pharynx. Planaria are sensitive to chemicals in the water. Special cells called **chemoreceptors** help them find food.

Reproduction

Planaria can reproduce by simply dividing and regenerating, or they can mate and lay eggs. Planaria, like all other flatworms, are hermaphrodites; each has both male and female sex organs. When two planaria mate, each transfers sperm to the other and both end up with fertilized eggs. Some species lay a number of eggs together in a capsule, or cocoon. The cocoons are attached to rocks and other objects by a small stalk. Eggs that are laid in the summer hatch in a couple of weeks. Those laid as winter approaches usually stay dormant until spring.

Taxonomy

PHYLUM: *Platyhelminthes (the flatworms)*

CLASS: *Trematoda (parasitic flukes), Cestoda (parasitic tapeworms), Turbellaria (free-living flatworms, 3000 species described. There are some parasitic and commensal turbellarians.)*

ORDER: *Tricladida (includes freshwater planaria)*

FAMILY: *Planariidae*

GENUS: *Dugesia (most common laboratory planarian. There are a number of other genera of freshwater planaria as well.)*

Commensalism

Some flatworms live on horseshoe crabs. Scientists consider these worms commensal, rather than parasitic, for though they live on the body of another animal, they do not seem to cause their host any harm.

Investigations with Planaria

Many kinds of planaria are easy to raise at home or in a lab. If you aren't able to collect wild planaria, you can order adults or eggs from a biological supply house (see page 124).

Raising planaria at home

Put a few planaria in a clean container. A shallow glass baking pan or casserole dish will work, as will a stainless steel or enameled pan. Plastic containers are too hard to keep clean. Fill the container with bottled spring water, or water from the place where you found the planaria. Don't use tap water; it may contain chemicals that are toxic to planaria. The water need not be deep; two inches is plenty. Add a few stones for the planaria to hide under.

Different species of planaria have different diets. In the wild, most eat tiny animals, and some feed on the bodies of animals that have recently died. Still others browse through the muck, eating whatever decaying plants and animals they find. At home, you can try feeding your planaria small pieces of liver or other raw meat. Some species will eat hard-boiled egg yolk. If these foods are rejected, you can try small worms or other live animals.

Give the planaria half an hour to feed, then remove leftover food. Rub your finger around the pan or dish to loosen any slime, and empty out the old, fouled water. Finish by filling the container with fresh water. Feed your planaria once a week.

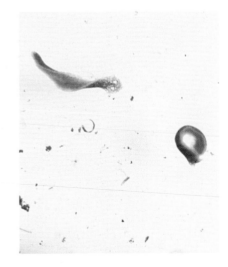

Regeneration

Most planaria can regenerate parts of their bodies. Growing back a missing part allows planaria to recover from injuries, and it's one way some species reproduce. This kind of reproduction is called **transverse fission**. It begins when a planarian's body starts to "pinch in" at the sides. A dividing line forms behind the pharynx. With its tail end holding onto the bottom, the head, or anterior end, of the planarian moves forward. Eventually, the two halves separate. Each regenerates the missing part, resulting in two half-old, half-new worms.

Regeneration has interested researchers who have discovered that if a planarian is deliberately cut in two across its middle, the tail end will grow a new head and the head end will grow a new tail. If one is divided lengthwise, the right half will grow a new left and vice-versa. To observe regeneration yourself, carefully cut a planarian in two with a single edged razor blade. Make note of where you make your cut, and make daily observations to see what changes occur. You will not need to feed regenerating planaria, but make sure to change their water every week.

Simple investigations

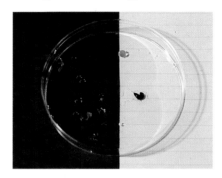

You can design simple experiments to find out more about planaria. For example, you can put them in a clear glass dish with dark paper under one half and light paper under the other. Do your planaria show a preference for one background over the other? You can also darken half of the container with a paper cover to see if they prefer light or dark areas. How do planaria respond to a current of water squirted out of an eye dropper? Do they respond differently when you direct a current at their heads than they do when you direct one at their sides or tail ends?

Research on flatworms

Barbara Boyer is doing research on the flatworm *Hoploplana*. She observes the way its eggs divide and develop into embryos, in order to better understand how the different ways that organisms develop have evolved. Scientists have noticed that some animals develop in similar ways. For example, if a cell is destroyed while an annelid, arthropod, or mollusc egg is dividing, the resulting embryo will lack the particular parts destined to grow from that cell. This is partly true of *Hoploplana*. Boyer has learned that it is not possible to predict exactly which structures will be missing when a particular cell is destroyed.

37

Explore the World of Birds

You can find birds just about everywhere on the Earth. Some dive after fish in the chilly waters of the Antarctic Ocean, while others hunt snakes and lizards in the desert. Some build their nests behind waterfalls, others prefer caves, and still others raise families on top of tall city buildings. They range in size from hummingbirds so small they are sometimes confused for insects to ostriches that stand taller than a person. In fact, there are more than 8,700 different species of birds that we know about. But as different as they are, all birds have some very important things in common, including:

- *Feathers:* Birds are the only animals that have feathers.
- *Two legs and two wings:* All birds walk on their two legs and feet an have two wings. Even birds that don't fly, like penguins, still have a pair of wings.
- *Bills or beaks:* All birds have these special mouthparts, which never have teeth, and they don't chew up their food like we do.
- *Eggs:* All birds hatch from eggs.

The scientists who keep track of all these facts about birds (and many, many others) are called ornithologists, and this chapter has lots of projects that will let you study birds the way they do. You'll learn to identify birds by their shapes, colors, and calls (p. 42) and their nests (p. 52). You'll study the diet of owls by dissecting the pellets that they produce after eating (p. 48). To study the 21-day life cycle of chicken eggs, you'll incubate and hatch baby chicks (p. 50). And to continue your bird studies, you can build a bird observation station in your backyard (p. 56). You don't need much equipment to study birds, but page 124 has information on ordering binoculars, incubators, and field guides, which you might find useful.

GETTING STARTED

Begin your study of birds by finding some birds to watch. They don't need to be any special kind; in fact, you don't even need to know what kind they are! If you watch them closely for a while, you will discover many things about how they look and what they do.

Birds sometimes nest in ivy on walls.

Where to go, what to bring

Birds live just about everywhere. You can find them in city parks, suburban back yards, vacant lots, and parking lots. Make your first field trip to a part of your neighborhood where you remember seeing birds, or where you think birds would be likely to live. You don't need to bring any special equipment with you. Your first trip can be a time to discover where birds can be found in your neighborhood, and to see how many you can spot. Plan to wear comfortable clothing that suits the weather and the area where you will walk. Wear long pants if you plan to go through tall weeds or brush, especially if ticks are common where you live. Tuck your pant legs into your socks for added protection from ticks.

Birds at a distance

Many of the birds you see will be far away, or will fly off when they first notice you. Watch them any-way. Even if you aren't able to get a good look at the color of their feathers, or see them for long, you can still notice many important things. Try to describe the way they fly through the air, and listen for their songs.

Some birds can soar through the air, rarely moving their wings. Others hover, or fly with deep, steady wing beats, or flap and then glide.

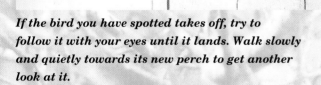

If the bird you have spotted takes off, try to follow it with your eyes until it lands. Walk slowly and quietly towards its new perch to get another look at it.

Birds up close

Some birds, like pigeons and herring gulls, are used to living among people, and you will be able to watch them at close range. Take a good look at the colors of their feathers, and the way they walk and use their wings. You can often get close to shyer birds as well. Just walk to a place where you will be comfortable sitting or standing for a few minutes, then stay as still and quiet as you can. Birds that were alarmed when you first approached will often come out of hiding once you stop moving around, and will walk or fly quite near you.

Binoculars

Although binoculars are not absolutely necessary for birdwatching, many people like to use them because they can give a close-up view of birds that are far away. If you do not already own binoculars but are thinking about getting a pair, try out a friend's to see what using them is like. There are many different binoculars on the market, so talk to experienced birdwatchers to find out what type they find easiest to use. Most birdwatchers use binoculars that have a wide field of view, and are able to magnify an image about seven or eight times. Binoculars with a central focusing knob are easiest to use. Some birdwatchers also use special telescopes called spotting scopes to look at birds (See page 124 for information on ordering binoculars.)

Think about timing

Try looking for birds at different times of the day. Some birds start singing before dawn, while others hunt at night. Many birds are most active early in the morning. If you have trouble finding birds in your neighborhood, schedule a bird walk at sunrise.

You may find you can get a closer look at small birds that are hidden among tree branches if you make a sharp "pssh-pssh-pssh" sound. Some birds will hop out to the ends of branches and look around when they hear this sound.

41

Identifying Birds

I t's fun to watch birds, whether you know what to call them or not. Often, though, you will want to identify the birds you see. Wild birds can be tricky to identify. They are often on the move, so it can be hard to get a good, long look at them. Luckily, many birds have shapes, color patterns, and ways of behaving that you can learn to recognize at a glance.

When you spot a bird

When you first notice a bird, watch to see how it looks, and what it is doing. You may want to focus on it with your binoculars for a better view. Describe it to a friend, or just to yourself. Note the color, shape, and size of various parts, as well as your general impressions.. After the bird has flown away, or after you have studied it for a while, jot down your description in a notebook, and make a quick sketch of the bird. Your careful observations and notes will help you recognize the bird if you ever see another like it. You won't always get a good look at every aspect of a bird. For example, if the light is poor, a bird's colors may not show up. Don't worry; just describe whatever you *can* see. You will soon be able to recognize many species based on a few important aspects of their appearance.

Using a field guide

A field guide can help you identify the birds you see. Field guides to the birds contain pictures of different birds, and short descriptions about their habits. They point out **field marks**, or details of a bird's appearance that can help you identify it at a distance. Many guides also have **range maps** that show where each species usually lives.

After you have looked carefully at a bird and described it to yourself, you can see if any of the pictures in your field guide look similar. Compare your own description of the bird with the pictures in your guide that most closely match what you saw. Check the range maps to see if the birds listed in your guide live in the area where you have been birdwatching. Also read the text, and check the measurements and behaviors it describes against your own observations.

Identifying birds can be difficult. An individual may be a little larger, darker, or more brightly colored than the one pictured in your guide. Or you may see a bird that has wandered far from the place where it usually lives. You may have to make observations over time, or consult an experienced birdwatcher, in order to identify some of the birds you see.

Jot down descriptions and make sketches of the birds you see.

Other ways to identify birds

Even ornithologists find some birds difficult to identify! Certain warblers look so much alike that researchers can only tell them apart by looking at their nests, and some small flycatchers are most easily distinguished by their songs. In fact, some birds, like owls and whippoorwills, are often heard but seldom seen. You can buy a tape recording of bird songs, or check one out from your library.

One species or two? Or three?

When you first begin to study birds, it may be hard to tell if you are looking at two members of the same species, or two completely different birds. This is because many kinds of birds look a lot alike, even though they have different habits and never mate with one another. Sometimes members of a single species can confuse us, because their appearance may change with the seasons, or as they grow older. Further, the male members of a species may not have the same colors and markings as the females. Keep track of the different birds you see by sketching or photographing them, and writing short descriptions. Your notes will help you remember what you have seen, and make good use of field guides and other references.

You can see this catbird's black cap and gray body; it also has a patch of chestnut feathers on its back.

Field marks, like the red forehead of this male house finch, can help you identify a bird that is partly hidden.

Young robins, like this one, have speckled breasts. As they get older, their breasts turn dark red.

The crest on the head of this Northern cardinal is a striking feature and easy to spot, even in poor light.

Two members of the same species may look quite different. In the summertime, male goldfinches have bright yellow bodies, while females are olive-yelow. In the winter, both sexes are olive-yellow.

Birds have different shapes, or **silhouettes***, that can help you recognize them at a distance.*

How Birds Are Built

irds have bodies that are like ours in some ways, but very different in others. Next time you are close to a bird, study the way its body is "put together." Think about the features all birds have in common, and how different species are adapted for life in particular kinds of places. Pet stores, zoos, and nature centers that keep some birds in cages are good places to study bird bodies. Caged birds can't fly far, so you will be able to get a good look at them.

Made to fly

Most birds are built to fly. They have streamlined bodies that move easily through the air, lightweight skeletons, and strong muscles to power their wings. Birds have backbones that are fused together (unlike ours, which allow our backs to bend and wiggle). This keeps a bird's body stiff as it moves through the air. Feathers provide lightweight insulation, as well as contribute to the streamlined body shape.

Birds have **tendons** that connect the bones of their lower legs and feet to muscles in the "thigh" and "drumstick," so they are able to move their lower legs and feet without a lot of heavy muscle. Different species of birds have different kinds of feet. Some feet can get a good grip on prey, while others are good for swimming, wading, or perching.

Eyes and ears

Birds have well-developed eyes, and very keen eyesight. In this owl skull, the eye sockets seem to take up most of the skull! Birds' brains have a large **optic lobe** that processes information from the eyes.

Most birds have eyes on the sides of their heads. This allows them to see what is in front of them, and to each side, and some of what is behind them–all at once! Owls have both eyes facing front, as we do.

An owl's skull.

This gives owls good **depth perception**, that is, they can judge distances accurately. However, it limits their **field of vision**, or how far around they can see. Birds have eyelids, and they also have a transparent **nictating membrane** that can quickly move across the eye to moisten and clean it.

Birds have ears, one on each side of their heads. The ears don't show, because they are covered with a layer of feathers and birds don't have **external ears** that stick out from the body. Birds have a highly developed sense of hearing.

All birds have a beak or bill. Bills come in many shapes and sizes. Herons have long, sturdy bills that enable them to grab fish and frogs out of the water, while sparrows have short bills that can pick up insects and crack open seeds. A hummingbird's bill can reach deep into flowers and suck out nectar, while a woodpecker can peck into tree bark. Shorebirds have sensitive beaks that can feel for prey in the sand.

A bird has two nostrils in its beak that connect to air passages that lead to lungs.

All mammals, including people, have seven small neck bones called **vertebrae**. Different species of birds, however, have different numbers of neck bones. Herons have 16 or 17, and swans have up to 25!

NICTATING MEMBRANE   SMALL EARHOLE   BEAK AND TONGUE   NOSTRILS   MANY VERTEBRAE

45

Reconstructing a chicken wing

One way to learn more about a bird's body is to study the skin, muscles, and bones of a chicken from the grocery store. Buy a whole chicken, instead of one that is already cut into pieces, so that you can see how the wings and legs attach to the body, and how they bend. You will see pores on the skin where feathers once grew. These form lines, called feather tracts. You can also see that the chicken's breast, or "white meat," contains large, powerful muscles that move the wings.

Directions:

1. After you have looked over the whole chicken, get help to cut one wing off.
2. Cook the wing in a pot of water until the skin and meat become soft.
3. Remove the wing and let it cool. (You can save the broth in the pot to make soup with if you want.)
4. Pull as much of the skin and bone off the wing as you can. Then return the bones to the pot and cook them a while longer.
5. Remove the bones from the pot and cool them.
6. Use an old toothbrush to scrub off any remaining bits of muscle.
7. Study the different bones, then reassemble them on a piece of cardboard. You can use white glue to fix them in place.
8. If you wish, you can label the bones.

The bones in a bird's wing are similar to the bones in our arms. The thickest bone in the chicken's wing is called the **humerus**. The part of a bird's wing that contains the humerus is the part that joins the bird's body. (Your own humerus is in your upper arm, and stretches from your shoulder to your elbow.) The **radius** and **ulna** are the two slender bones that attach to the humerus. (These bones are in your

lower arm, between your elbow and wrist.) Because there are two bones in our lower arm, we can rotate this part of our body. Birds are able to rotate the middle section of their wings, too. The small bones in the "end" part of a bird's wing are similar to the bones in our wrist and hand.

Next time you see a bird in flight, think about what the bones inside its wings are like, and how they allow the wings to move.

Beach Bird Food

Though it is easy to watch shorebirds feeding, it is often hard to see just what it is they collect with their bills. You can find out what food is available to them, though, by searching through the sand and shallow water. Look for beach bird food in areas where you have noticed birds feeding.

Equipment you will need:
- plastic shovel or garden trowel
- sieve or strainer
- plastic bucket

Directions:
1. Choose a part of the beach where you have seen birds feeding.
2. Look for marine animals around rocks, and in piles of seaweed. Save a sample of each kind of "food" in your bucket.
3. Look through shallow water to the sand below. You might find clues, such as lugworm castings or the siphon holes of clams, that tell you animals are buried there.
4. Dig up some sand or mud. You only need to dig as deep as a shorebird, so think about how long the beaks are on the birds you have seen.
5. Place the sand or mud in your sifter or strainer. Gently swirl it in shallow water to strain the sand out.
6. Once the sand and mud have been washed away, check to see what animals remain.

Look carefully in areas where you see shorebirds feeding to discover what they eat. Different species eat different prey.

CLAM SIPHON HOLE

Animals you might find in the sand:

- Clams

- Clam worms

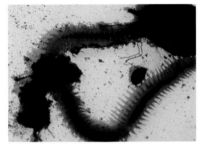

- Lugworms (casting)

- Trumpet worms

- Mole crabs

Animals you might find on rocks, or in piles of seaweed:

- Periwinkles

- Barnacles

- Mussels

An ancient food supply

For millions of years, horseshoe crabs have been laying their eggs along what is now the east coast of the United States. Pairs of crabs swim ashore beginning in May, and the females lay thousands of eggs in nests in the sand. The eggs are laid at high tide during the highest high tides, or **spring tides**. Over the days that follow, the tides will continue to ebb and flow, but the water will not rise as far up on the beach as it did during these spring tides. Instead of washing away, the horseshoe crab eggs are able to develop in the sandy nests. After a month they will hatch, and a new round of spring tides will wash them into the sea. That is, *some* of them will be washed to sea. Many eggs will never survive long enough to hatch. Instead, they will disappear into the bellies of gulls and shorebirds. Horseshoe crab eggs are an important source of food for shorebirds on their way north to breeding grounds in the Arctic.

Ornithologists can't always know for sure what birds have been eating simply by watching them. Sometimes, they dissect birds and examine the contents of their stomachs. Some birds vomit up **pellets** that contain undigestible parts of the things they have eaten. Scientists also study these pellets.

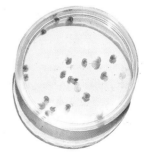

Young horseshoe crabs (above) and the shed "skin" of an adult horseshoe crab (left).

What Owls Eat

If you've ever been near the woods at night, you may have heard an owl call. Each species has a distinctive call, so it is possible to find out what kinds of owls live near you just by listening. All owls are predators, but since different species have different diets, more than one kind of owl may live in a particular woodland without competing for the same food.

Great horned owls prey on rabbits and other small animals.

You may find that the easiest way to get a good, close look at an owl is to visit a museum.

What owls eat

Great horned owls hunt for mice, rabbits, and other small mammals in the woods at night. Though mammals are their principal food, they also eat beetles, frogs, lizards, and birds. Barred owls eat small mammals, too, though in southern swampy woodlands crayfish, frogs, and fish are the mainstays of their diet. The smaller screech owl usually feeds on insects.

How did people figure out what these nocturnal hunters eat? Some people have actually observed owls at night, and seen them catch and eat prey. People also learn about animal diets by examining droppings and **pellets**. Owls tend to swallow their prey whole, or to tear off and gulp down large pieces. When an owl eats a mouse, it swallows it—fur, bones, and all. The fur and bones aren't nutritious or digestible, however, and they are regurgitated, or thrown up, a few hours later, pressed together in a pellet.

You might find an owl pellet when you are walking in the woods. Sometimes a few will be piled up under an owl's favorite perch. You can also buy pellets to study. Wildlife centers that rehabilitate injured owls often collect them from captive birds.

Dissecting an owl pellet

1. If your pellet is dry, soak it in water for a few minutes to soften the fur and feathers.

2. Use your fingers, toothpicks, or a probe and forceps to gently tease apart the pellet.

3. Separate bones, teeth, and other hard material from soft fur and feathers and clean them with a damp sponge.

4. You can use a book about bones, or a field guide to mammals, to help you identify some of the bones you find.

5. Mount the bones on poster board or construction paper, or try to reconstruct a skeleton from bones that seem like they might have come from the same animal.

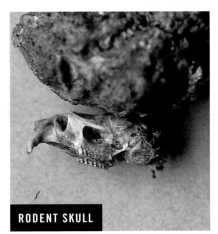

RODENT SKULL

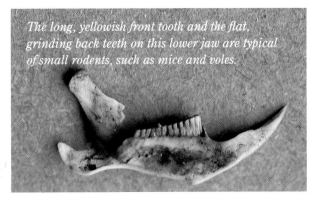

The long, yellowish front tooth and the flat, grinding back teeth on this lower jaw are typical of small rodents, such as mice and voles.

Hatching Chickens

 Bird eggs will only hatch if they are kept at the proper temperature. In the wild, adult birds care for their eggs in various ways. Some birds, like the Egyptian plover, bury their eggs in the sand to keep them from getting too hot. Others, like the American robin, sit on their eggs to incubate them, or keep them warm. The emperor penguin carries its single egg about on its feet, incubating it under a fold of belly skin. If you want to hatch baby birds, you will need an incubator and some fertilized eggs. Domestic chicken eggs are usually the easiest to come by.

Setting up an incubator

An **incubator** is a special box that can be kept warm inside with a heating cable. Incubators are expensive, so check to see if a local school, nature center, or Cooperative Extension Service has one you can borrow. If you can't borrow one, see page 124 for information on ordering one from a supply house.

Set up your incubator in a draft-free area, away from direct sunlight. Place a thermometer on the wire platform in the bottom of the incubator, so you can monitor the temperature inside.

Plug in the incubator the day before you pick up the eggs, so that the climate inside the incubator can stabilize. Check the incubator frequently during the day, so you can adjust the temperature and humidity if necessary. Chicken eggs are incubated at 100–101 degrees F. If your thermometer registers a warmer or cooler temperature, adjust the

With a heating cable and some water, this incubator simulates the moist warmth of a hen's nest.

control on the thermostat. Moisture is also important for developing eggs, so put a pan of water under the wire platform to humidify the air. Once the temperature and humidity in the incubator have stabilized within the proper range, you are ready to add the eggs.

Getting eggs

You will need fresh, **fertile** chicken eggs to put in your incubator. Grocery store eggs won't do, because they are usually not fertile. The hens that laid them did not mate with roosters, so chicks will never develop inside these eggs. You may be able to get fertile eggs at a farm. If you don't live near a farm, call a local museum, nature center, or Cooperative Extension Service to find out where you can get eggs. If you do not have space at home to raise a flock of chickens, make arrangements for the chicks before you buy eggs. The farmer who sold you the eggs may be happy to raise the chickens.

Incubating the eggs— the first 18 days

Chicken eggs take 21 days to hatch. During this period, hens spend a lot of time sitting on their eggs to keep them warm. They also roll the eggs around with their beaks every now and then, which keeps the developing **embryos** from sticking to the **membrane**, or skin-like material that lines the shell. You will need to turn the eggs in your incubator, too. Simply open the incubator, and roll each egg over. If you mark each egg with a pencil "X" on one side, it will be easy to make sure you have turned all of the eggs completely. Turn the eggs three or four times a day until the 18th day of incubation—then leave them alone! They need to sit still during the three days before hatching.

Check the temperature and humidity before you open the incubator to turn the eggs. If the temperature drops even a few degrees below 100, the embryos will develop slowly. If the temperature rises above 103 degrees, they may be killed. Adjust the thermostat and water pans as necessary.

Days 19–21

During the last few days of incubation, you will need to care differently for the eggs. Each chick embryo will have moved into a hatching position within its eggshell, with its head at the large end of the egg. It is important to stop turning the eggs at this point, so the position of the chicks will not be disrupted. Leave the incubator closed at all times, so it will stay humid.

Don't forget to turn your eggs, or they won't develop properly.

On the 21st day, start looking for signs of hatching. You may hear peeping sounds coming from inside an egg, or notice a tiny hole in the middle of an eggshell. A **pipping** chick will push at the eggshell with its **egg tooth**, and crack little holes around its middle. Eventually, the chick will push the two halves of the eggshell apart and be free of them.

Some chicks take many hours to hatch, and it is tempting to open the incubator and help them! However, it is important to leave the incubator closed, and let the chicks do their

own work. That way, you won't accidentally hurt a tiny chick by handling it, and the air in the incubator will stay warm and moist, so the chicks will not stick to their eggshells.

Leave each chick in the incubator until it looks dry and fluffy. Then you can take it out of the incubator and move it to a **brooder** that is warmed to about 90 degrees by a 60 watt light bulb. Keep an eye on the chicks in the brooder to see how they are managing. If they constantly huddle under the light, they may be too cold, and you will need to adjust the light to bring it closer to the box. If the chicks avoid the light completely, the box may be too hot. Feed young chicks starter mash from a feed store or corn meal, and make sure their waterer is always full.

Move your chicks to a brooder once they are dry.

Watching Nests

ext time you spot a bird carrying grass or a twig in its beak, watch to see where the bird goes. You may be able to locate the nest it is building. Keep track of the nest over the season to see how the adult bird cares for its young.

Observing an active nest

Start looking for active nests in the spring. Check around your home or school building—some birds nest under eaves and ledges, over doorways, and in other protected nooks and crannies. Once you locate a nest, observe it often. Try to move slowly and quietly when you are near the nest, and keep your distance at first. Some nesting birds are easily disturbed by people, and may abandon their eggs if they feel threatened by your visit. Binoculars will allow you to observe these birds from a safe distance. Few birds will abandon their chicks once the eggs have hatched.

Ornithologists use special, long-handled mirrors to get a look at nests they can't see from the ground. You can make your own nest-viewer by attaching a dime-store mirror to a pole or broom handle. Fasten the mirror securely so it will not fall off and break, or slip and bump a nest when you are using it. Try looking at abandoned nests, tree branches, and other high objects before you attempt to view an active nest. It may take some practice to learn to position the mirror so

you can see exactly what you want to.

You can make brief nest observations with your mirror whenever the adult birds have flown off to get food. If an adult is actually on its nest, **incubating** the eggs, or waiting nearby with food for the chicks, save your mirror for another time so that the adult can continue to take care of its young.

What's in a nest?

It is fascinating to see how different species of birds construct their nests, and what materials they use to make them. Start looking for abandoned nests to study in late fall, when birds no longer need them. You may be able to see many of the nest materials that were used by inspecting the surface of a nest. You can also take a nest apart bit by bit,

A piece of string, a bit of green cellophane, and some red wool were woven into this nest of twigs and grasses.

and take a more exact inventory. Sort the materials into piles, and see if there are any you can recognize. Take a small sample from each pile back to the area where you found the nest, and see if you can find a place where the nest-maker might have collected it. Some birds make many trips to a particular area to gather the materials they need for their nests.

The red-eyed vireo builds a hanging nest in the fork of a slender, horizontal branch.

Identifying nests

If you were able to observe a nest when it was active, you can simply identify the nest by identifying the birds you saw using it. If you spot a nest for the first time after it has been abandoned, a field guide or a key to the nests typically found in your area may help you figure out what kind of bird made it. Make sure to note the location of the nest. Some birds are particular about their nest sites, and tend to build in certain kinds of trees, or at a certain

height. Also look to see what the nest is made of, what its basic shape is, and whether it is loosely constructed or finely woven. If it is attached to a plant or building, look to see how it is attached. It may also help to measure the height of the nest, the depth of the cup, the **outside diameter** (the distance across the entire nest), and the **inside diameter** (the distance from one side of the hollow cup to the other). You can compare these measurements to those given in your field guide.

Studying nests

You can learn a lot from studying abandoned nests up close. However, in the United States, it is against federal regulations to collect the nest of any migratory bird or endangered species.

Educators, scientists, and other people who are interested in birds often obtain special permits to collect and study nests, feathers, or live birds. They can often provide you with nests to study. You can also contact the U.S. Fish and Wildlife Service in your area to find out if you will need a permit for your work.

Bird Songs and Calls

The sounds birds make are a familiar—and often beautiful—part of our daily lives, and they have special meaning for many people. Flocks of honking geese tell us winter is on the way, and forecast spring's return. Owls can sound spooky, and mourning doves sad. Bird sounds are a form of communication. However, the meaning they have for us can be quite different from the meaning they carry for birds! It takes careful watching and listening, as well as some imagination, to figure out what a bird is "saying."

Calls and songs

Birds make different kinds of sounds. Calls are usually short, simple sounds, and they are made by males, females, and young birds. An individual can make a variety of different calls, and each sends a partic- ular message to other birds. When a nestling peeps, for example, its parents feed it. The peeping seems to say "Feed me!" Ducklings often call as they swim or walk near their mother, and their mother calls back. These calls probably help a family of ducks stay in touch with one another, as if each member were continually saying "Here I am—over here." If one duckling gets separated from the group, it calls more loudly and frequently. Its mother responds to its **distress call** by coming near. The

honking calls of migrating Canada geese may serve a similar purpose— they help the members of a flock stay together, but not so near they might collide. Birds call at all times of the year. Their calls can help members of a family or flock recognize one another, sound an alarm when danger is near, or warn intruders away from a territory, perch, or feeding area. The "language" of a particular species may include as many as twenty–five distinct calls! Listen closely to the birds that are most common in your neighborhood, and see how many different calls you can recognize.

Bird songs are usually longer and more complicated than calls. Each species has a distinct song, and you can learn to recognize it by particular note patterns, or phrases, that are repeated each time the song is sung. You will hear different variations of a species' song, though, because one individual may sing a little differently than another, or sing many versions of the same basic song. Of course, a bird can recognize its species' song, too, and use it to identify members of its own species. Most singing birds are males. During the breeding season, a male's song may attract a mate, or help him establish and maintain his territory. Early in the season, some males spend half of each day singing, and repeat their songs over a thousand—or even two thousand—times! The females of some species also sing, but they do not sing as often as males do. In some species, males and females sing duets. Many birds seem to know their songs instinctively; they can sing the song typical of their species even if they have never heard it before. Others learn their songs.

Ways to learn about bird songs and calls

- Go for an early morning bird walk, and see how many different sounds you can hear. Try listening at other times of day, as well, for some birds are noisiest in the evening, or at night.
- Keep track of the time of year when you hear a particular song. This will help you learn when various species are breeding.
- When you hear a bird song or call, try to find the bird that made it. Watch to see how other birds nearby respond. Over time, you may be able to figure out what sounds are made by a particular species, and what they mean.
- Check out a tape recording of bird songs from your public library, or buy one. If you hear a familiar song, you can listen to find out what bird made it. You can look at a field guide as you listen to the tape, and match up the way birds look with the way they sound.

- Try making your own bird recordings with a portable tape recorder. You'll get the best results with nearby birds that make relatively loud sounds.
- Describe the bird songs you hear in a notebook. Some people find that putting words to bird songs helps them remember and recognize them. The white-throated sparrow sounds as if it's singing "Oh, Sweet, Canada Canada Canada" or "Oh, Sam, Peabody Peabody Peabody," while the Carolina wren says "Teacher teacher teacher," and the barred owl asks "Who cooks for you?"
- Some birds will respond when you imitate their songs with your voice or a wooden bird call. Birds may respond to tape recorded songs as well. (See page 124 for information on ordering wooden bird calls.

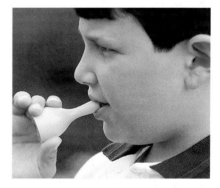

Feeding Birds

Birds are big eaters. Keeping warm in winter, flying, and nest building are activities that burn up a lot of calories! One way to get a good look at birds is to set up a feeding station. Birds are always on the lookout for new food supplies. Once they discover your feeding station, many will become regular visitors.

SUNFLOWER SEEDS

SUET

Setting up a station

First, decide where to locate your feeding station. If possible, put it where you can easily see it from your house or apartment. That way, it will be easy to maintain, and you will be able to observe the birds that visit whether you are indoors or out.

Next, decide what kind of feeders you will put up. There are dozens of different bird feeders on the market, and many more that you can build yourself. Some can be filled with seed and placed on a pole, or hung from a wire or window. Others hold **suet**, or fat. Still others are made to sit on the ground and hold cracked grain, crumbs, and seeds. Since birds have varied diets and feeding habits, you will attract the widest variety of species if you set up different kinds of feeders.

A simple feeding station can include:
- one hanging feeder full of sunflower seeds
- a lump of suet in an old plastic mesh onion bag
- cracked corn scattered on the ground.
- a piece of wood with holes filled with peanut butter

Talk to neighbors who have managed to attract birds before you spend a lot of money buying new feeders. They may have found some that work particularly well, and are easy to clean. (You will need to clean out your feeders and wash them periodically, especially if rainy weather wets the food.) Once your station is established, you can experiment with different kinds of food and feeders to see which attract the most birds. Keep track of the species that visit each feeder. (For more information on ordering feeders, see page 124.)

CRACKED CORN

PEANUT BUTTER

56

Some food birds eat

- sunflower seeds
- other seeds, such as millet, oats, wheat, and safflower seeds
- cracked corn
- chopped nuts
- suet
- peanut butter
- fruit (orioles and tanagers are attracted to orange halves)
- sugar water (hummingbirds)
  These foods are available at grocery stores, feed stores, and from mail order companies.

Squirrel-proofing your station

Birds aren't the only animals that eat sunflower seeds and cracked corn! If you don't want squirrels and chipmunks to eat from your feeders, make sure to put them on metal poles instead of wooden ones, or hang them from a wire strung between two poles. This will make it difficult for squirrels and chipmunks to reach your feeders. You can also buy plastic "squirrel-bafflers" to fit many feeders. Of course, there's no way to keep squirrels away from the food you scatter on the ground, so see what you can learn about them when they come to eat.

Perches and hiding places

Birds are more likely to feed at your station if there are plenty of places nearby where they can perch, and places to take cover if a person, cat, or hawk surprises them. Fences, poles, shrubs, trees, and tall weeds can provide perches and cover. If your feeding station is in a bare or exposed area, try planting tall flowers or shrubs close by. Pound a few poles or fence posts into the ground, or scatter a few large, dead branches around. You can also prop large branches against a fence post to support them. They will provide food for woodpeckers and other birds that search tree bark for insects to eat, as well as offer places to perch.

Water

Birds need water as well as food. If you have an old birdbath, set it up at your station. If not, you can weight a shallow tray or garbage can lid with a rock, and keep it full of fresh water.

Hummingbirds feed on the nectar from flowers, but you can also attract them with sugar water.

Living at the Seashore

When most of us go to the sea, it's for a quick visit, to swim in it or sail on it or surf on its waves or even just to look at and listen to it. Some people, like fishermen and sailors, spend more of their time in the sea, but they still don't get to see much of it beyond the very top where they float. But oceans cover more than three-quarters of the Earth, and are home to many, many kinds of plants and animals, quite a lot more than live on land with us. The scientists who study these plants and animals are marine biologists. They study everything from blue whales, the biggest animals of all time, to the tiny, one-celled plankton that these whales eat.

It can be a little complicated getting out to the middle of an ocean, but the edges of the oceans, the beaches and shorelines, are easier to visit and just as full of fascinating creatures. This chapter is full of projects and experiments that you can do at beaches to discover more about the world of seashore life. You'll learn how to find animals that live in the sand (p. 62), how to collect and "read" the information on seashells (p. 64), and how to press, preserve, and identify different kinds of seaweed (p. 78). If you'd like to be able to temporarily house your beach finds, you can learn how to set up your own salt water aquarium at home (p. 74). And there are plenty of animals you can order from the list on page 124 or from your local pet store if you don't live near enough to a beach to go yourself.

But always remember: the sea is not our natural environment and we have to be very careful around it. Never go in the water by yourself, and always tell an adult where you are going.

THE SANDY SHORE

Each stretch of sandy shoreline is unique, or unlike any other. There are protected bays with gently moving water, and exposed beaches where the surf pounds fiercely. Many plants and animals inhabit quiet, sandy shallows. In rough waters, where pounding waves are constantly stirring up the sand, it is more difficult for marine plants and animals to live. But even on exposed beaches, you can learn a lot about what lives in the sea. Shells, bones, and other remains of marine plants and animals are carried onshore from deeper water. Burrowing creatures find a stable environment underneath the shifting sand. Dig around. Get your feet wet. See what you can find.

60

What to bring

A plastic bucket makes a good temporary aquarium when you want to observe an animal for a while before letting it go. You can also use the bucket to transport live specimens to a saltwater aquarium you may have set up at home.

Old sneakers or reef shoes will keep your feet safe from jagged rocks and broken shells and glass.

A plastic hand lens will give you a close-up view of the plants and animals you find.

A small shovel will help you unearth animals that are buried in the sand.

Bring a net to scoop small fish, crabs, and jellyfish from calm shallows.

Ways to look

Sort through the piles of eelgrass, seaweed, and other debris that have been left by recent high tides. You may find fish bones, feathers, seashells, or the egg case of a skate. Wade through the wash. Examine pieces of seaweed to see what kinds have drifted in, and whether any shrimp-like **amphipods**, marine snails, or eggs are clinging to them. Dig in the sandy shallows, and turn over stray rocks. Marine worms, crustaceans, and shellfish often inhabit these protected places. Make sure to replace rocks and sand so the organisms that live on and under them will survive.

Buried Treasure

Many marine animals use specially adapted body parts to tunnel into wet sand. Living down under the sand, instead of on its surface, protects them from the constant motion of waves, from drying winds that would otherwise reach them at low tide, and from predators. Use a small shovel or plastic container to search for these animals. Scoop up sand, then sift through it with your fingers or a strainer to see what you've caught.

Clams

Mercenaria mercenaria uses its strong foot to dig down into the sand. Once buried, it eats tiny organisms it filters out of the water with its gills. These gills are coated with slimy mucus that moves particles of trapped food towards the clam's mouth. A clam's gills are inside its shell. Seawater is pulled into them through the **inhalent siphon**, a special tube the clam can stick up through the sand. A second tube, called the **exhalent siphon**, pumps filtered water back out.

   Mercenaria mercenaria, also known as the quahog, littleneck, or hard-shell clam, can be found along

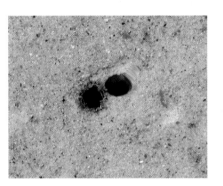

much of the east coast of North America and in some parts of California. Many other marine clams feed the same way *Mercenaria* does. You can spot their siphon holes in the sand when the tide is low and the water is calm. Razor clams are the hardest to catch. They burrow with amazing speed, and can also use their long feet to swim.

Clam eaters

Clams are eaten by moon snails, oyster drills, shorebirds, starfish, and people. Clam worms, like members of the genus *Nereis*, include dead clams in their diet.

Look for them under rocks or buried in the sand during the day, or search the shallows with a flashlight after dark. Handle them carefully; they can bite!

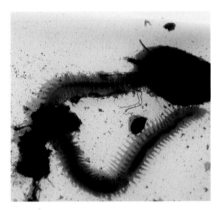

The clam worm, Nereis viriens, *should be handled carefully. It feeds on dead clams, but may bite you, too.*

Mole crabs

Mole crabs are small **crustaceans** with curved backs and short legs. Unlike other crabs, they don't have claws. Instead, their legs are adapted for digging. Mole crabs move in and out with the tide, staying right near the line where waves break. Over and over again they bury themselves in the sand, are unearthed by waves, and bury themselves again. They eat the tiny algae floating in the water and packed between sand grains. The Atlantic mole crab, *Emerita talpoida*, can be found from Cape Cod to Mexico. It lives near shore during the warmer months, and spends the winter offshore where it is not in danger of freezing. The Pacific mole crab, *Emerita analoga*, lives in a range that extends from Alaska to Peru.

Sand dollars

Sand dollars, like their relatives the sea urchins, are covered with spines. The spines can move, and a sand dollar buries itself by moving its spines back and forth. Most sand dollars don't move very fast, or very far. They feed on algae and tiny particles of organic matter mixed in with the sand. Look for their mouths on the underside of their bodies, right in the middle. When sand dollars die, their spines fall off. You may find their round, flat skeletons, or **tests**, washed up on the beach.

Echinarachnius parma, *a common sand dollar, can be found from Alaska to Puget Sound in the Pacific, and from Labrador to Maryland in the Atlantic.*

Trumpet worms

Pectinaria gouldii, the trumpet or ice cream cone worm, builds itself a case out of sand grains. It uses the golden **setae** on its head to dig a U-shaped tunnel in the sand, then "stands on its head" at one end of the tunnel. It collects pieces of food from the water that passes through its tunnel, and its wastes are carried to the surface. *Pectinaria gouldii* can be found in sandy mud along the east coast of the United States.

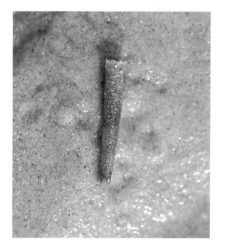

Taxonomy

Clams are in the phylum Mollusca, class Bivalvia.

Mole crabs are in the phylum Arthropoda, class Crustacea.

Clam worms and trumpet worms are in the phylum Annelida, class Polychaeta.

Sand dollars, like sea urchins and starfish, belong to the phylum Echinodermata. They share the class Echinoidea with sea urchins.

Collecting Shells

Walk along the beach, and sooner or later you'll find yourself picking up seashells. These beautiful structures were made, and once inhabited, by animals called **molluscs**. There are six classes of molluscs, but most of the shells you will find belong to the class Gastropoda or Bivalvia. Periwinkles, whelks, and other snail-like molluscs are **gastropods**. They make one-part, or **univalve**, shells. Clams, mussels, and scallops are **bivalve** molluscs; they make two-part shells. Often, the two parts separate after the animal inside dies.

It's easiest to find shells at low tide, when much of the beach is not covered by water. Try collecting after a storm. Large waves may have cast up shells you don't often see.

PHYLUM: *Mollusca*

CLASS: *Gastropoda*
SPECIES: *moon snail, whelk, periwinkle...*

CLASS: *Bivalvia*
SPECIES: *quahog, blue mussel, bay scallop...*

Making a collection

- Make sure shells are empty before you bring them home. Snails often draw their bodies into their shells and "close the door" by pulling the **operculum**, a flat piece of shell, over the opening. Hermit crabs, slipper shells, and barnacles may move in to empty shells they find. Leave shells that house living animals where you find them.
- Clean dirty specimens with soap, water, and an old toothbrush.

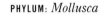

Look for hermit crabs, slipper shells, and other "shell collectors" on the beach.

- Mount your shells on a piece of cardboard or the bottom of a shallow box. Use white glue, and tuck a cotton ball under large or fragile specimens to help keep them from breaking. You can also keep shells in a plastic box subdivided into small compartments.
- Label each specimen. Record in a notebook the location where you collected it and the habits of the animal that made it. A field guide will help you identify your shells.

You may find other interesting things on the beach that you want to add to your shell collection. A horseshoe crab test (shed skin) and the empty egg case of a whelk are displayed here.

Shell stories

Though collectors often look for "perfect" specimens, damaged shells are just as interesting to study. You may be able to figure out part of a shell's life story from the kinds of holes or cracks it has.

A shell with a small, circular hole bored, or drilled, through it was probably eaten by a dogwinkle, oyster drill, or some other member of the family Murcidae. Also called "rock shells," these marine snails eat oysters, mussels, and other molluscs; they eat barnacles, too. Eating is slow work for a rock shell. It has to scrape a hole through the shell of its prey with its file-like **radula**, or tongue, to get at the soft body

inside. Since it preys on animals that are permanently attached to rocks or other shells, though, there's no need to hurry.

A pile of broken shells may mark the spot where a gull has been feeding. Gulls can't swallow large, hard shells. To get at the soft meat inside,

they drop shells onto rocks from the air, or hammer at them with their strong beaks.

Some sponges drill holes in old mollusc shells. The bodies of these sponges grow within the channels they make, and sometimes outgrow them as well. **Boring** sponges belong to the family Clionidae in the phylum Porifera. Shells that have housed boring sponges are usually full of holes.

Aging shells

You can estimate how long many of the clams, scallops, and other bivalves in your collection lived by counting their **annuli**, or yearly growth rings. This method of estimating age is only useful for shells with distinct annuli, so choose a shell with rings that show clearly. You will see many fine lines, or **circuli**, that were created as the animal grew and left minerals around the edge of its shell. The annuli are more well-defined than the circuli, and each marks the end of a major growth period. In many cases, this period equals one year.

The deep sea scallop, Placopecten megallanicus, *ranges from Labrador to Cape Cod, and as far south as North Carolina. They are often found washed up on the shore after storms.*

Hermit Crabs

People aren't the only shell collectors along the shore. The various hermit crabs that comprise the family Paguridae also hunt for shells in calm shallows.

Anatomy of a hermit crab

Most familiar seashore crabs have a hard **exoskeleton** covering their entire body. Hermit crabs are different. They have a hard **carapace** and legs towards the front, or **anterior**, end of their bodies, but their long, curving **abdomens** are soft. This is one feature that sets Pagurids apart from "true crabs" like blue and green crabs. Most hermit crabs protect their soft abdomens by placing them in abandoned mollusc shells. Two tiny hooks near the tip of their abdomens help them to hang on,

This crab lives in water, and belongs to the family Paguridae. Land hermit crabs, like those you might find in pet stores or on southern beaches, belong to the family Coenobitidae.

and they drag their borrowed shell with them wherever they go. You may be able to get a good look at a hermit crab's abdomen if you hold onto its shell for a minute or two. The crab is used to being able to move its shell, and may be unsettled enough by the change to leave its shell. After you've seen the way its body is shaped, lay the shell near the crab in your palm or in shallow water so the crab can get back in.

Moving day

Hermit crabs grow a great deal during their lives. Since the mollusc shells they inhabit don't grow, crabs must frequently trade in their old shells for new ones. This is fun to watch at the shore or in an aquarium. You may see a crab check the size of a new shell before actually trying it out by sticking its head and claws inside. Or you may see a crab

move into a new shell, only to reclaim its old one a moment later. Often, several crabs will fight over one shell. Sometimes other animals move onto the shells inhabited by hermit crabs. Sponges, slipper shells, and other **sessile** creatures seem to benefit by being carried around to new locations.

You can keep track of the moves a crab makes if you place it in a saltwater aquarium with empty mollusc shells of various shapes and sizes. Give each shell an identifying mark with nail polish. Make frequent observations to find out how often your crab moves, and whether it seems to prefer a particular kind of shell.

Taxonomy

PHYLUM:
Arthropoda
CLASS: *Crustacea*
ORDER: *Decapoda*
INFRAORDER: *Anomura*
("strange tails," or
crabs whose abdomens
don't "follow the rules")
FAMILY: *Paguridae*
(hermit crabs)
GENERA: *Pagurus (means*
"a crab"), as well as
Petrochirus,
Clibanarius, Dardanus
SPECIES: *The long-clawed*
hermit crab, Pagurus
longicarpus, and the
flat-clawed hermit crab,
Pagurus pollicaris, are
two common east coast
species. The grainy
hermit crab, Pagurus
granosimanus, the blue-
handed hermit crab,
Pagarus samuelis, and
the hairy hermit crab,
Pagarus hirsutiusculus,
are all wide-ranging
west coast species.

Food

Hermit crabs eat all kinds of dead animals and debris they find under-water. Sometimes they'll eat living animals as well, even other hermits. You can feed captive hermits small bits of fish or squid. They do well in clean, well-functioning saltwater aquaria, but will not survive long in buckets or jars of water. Be sure to set up a suitable habitat before you collect them! The instructions on pages 74–75 will help you do this.

If you're patient,
you may be able to coax
a hermit crab out of its shell.
Hold it in your hand to get a good
look at it, then offer it back its shell.

Clams

Clams spend most of their time buried in sand or mud. They use their strong, muscular foot to dig with. When you walk through the shallow water of a tidal flat or salt marsh, keep an eye out for siphon holes in the sand that tell you clams are below.

Clams, such as *Mercenaria mercenaria,* are **filter feeders**. Like many other aquatic animals, they eat the tiny plants, animals, and bits of decaying organic material suspended in the water. Unlike most other animals, they filter this food with their gills, the same organs they use to get oxygen out of the water. Clams eat to breathe, and breathe to eat. They can also get oxygen through their mantle, a layer of tissue just underneath the shell.

Water is pulled into a clam's body through the **inhalent siphon**, the one with a fringed end. The fringe helps keep sand and other debris out. After water is filtered, it is pumped back out through the **exhalent siphon**.

How old are you?

Mercenaria mercenaria starts out as a tiny, swimming larva, but as its shell and body grow, it buries itself in the sand. New shell is secreted by the mantle. As the clam gets larger, each **valve**, or half of its shell, grows around the edge. You can see lines that mark each season's growth, like the rings on a tree stump. You'll also notice a bump on each valve near its hinge. This bump, called the **umbo**, is the oldest part of the shell. By comparing the size of the umbo to the size of the entire shell,

Surf shell

Soft shell

you can see how much the clam has grown. You can also try estimating the age of a clam by counting its growth rings. Hard-shell clams like *Mercenaria* sometimes live twenty years or more!

Reproduction

Most clam species are dioecious; some are males and others female. Adults reproduce by pumping sperm or eggs out through their siphons. The eggs are fertilized in the water, then hatch into larvae. Some species, like the tiny "fingernail clams" you find in ponds, actually **brood** their eggs. The females keep their eggs inside their shells, on their gills. When males release sperm into the water, the females pull it in through their siphons. The fertilized eggs remain inside the female's shell until they hatch.

Dissecting a clam

Clams belong to the class Bivalvia, consisting of molluscs with a two-part shell. Mussels and oysters are also Bivalvia molluscs.

You can learn about the anatomy of **bivalve** molluscs by dissecting a clam. Buy one from a grocery store or fish market, or order a preserved specimen from one of the supply companies on page 124. A live clam will often close its shell tightly when removed from water. Freezing or boiling the clam will kill it and open its shell. Preserved specimens have to be opened by sliding a scalpel between the valves, and cutting through the two large muscles that clamp them together.

Inside you will see the large foot and the muscles that open and close the valves. You can also look for the gills, stomach, mantle, and **gonads**.

companies on page 124.

Taxonomy

PHYLUM: *Mollusca* (*soft-bodied marine animals*)
CLASS: *Bivalvia* (*molluscs with a two-part shell: clams, oysters, and mussels. Gills usually used for collecting food and getting oxygen.*)
SUBCLASS: *Lamellibranchia*
ORDER: *Heterodonta* (*fresh and saltwater clams, siphons usually present, a few large hinge teeth.*)
FAMILY: *Veneridae*
GENUS: *Mercenaria* (*common, edible marine clams*)
SPECIES: *Mercenaria mercenaria* (*quahog, or hard-shell clam*)

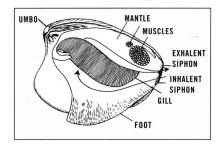

Once you have separated the valves, a clam's internal organs are easy to see.

Mya arenaria, *the steamer clam, cannot pull its siphons into its shell like many other clams can.*

69

Patterns within a Habitat:

 ost invertebrates are adapted for life in a particular **habitat**. But within a single habitat, conditions vary from place to place. Seemingly minor differences can cause an animal to find one spot livable, and another quite near it completely unsuitable. When you go looking for invertebrates, take note of where you find each one. You may discover that a particular species lives on or near a certain kind of plant, or that two different invertebrates are often found in close association with one another. Scientists are interested in these patterns.

Observing along a transect

You can set up a **transect** on a beach, in a field, or in your yard in order to find out more about invertebrate patterns in a particular area. Observing along a transect is like looking at a cross section of an area.

To begin, find a **transect site.** Choose one at random by closing your eyes, throwing an object, and locating the transect where it lands, or select a particular site that interests you. Set up a **benchmark** by driving a stake into the ground, or marking a rock with paint.

Run a length of clothesline marked off in yards through your benchmark. You now have a transect line running across your study site. With the benchmark as your "zero point," you can easily refer to other points along the transect. Positive numbers are used to label each yard marked on one side of the benchmark, and negative numbers are used on the other.

To develop a sense of where different invertebrates live, place a wooden frame or plastic hula hoop

along the transect at various points. At each point, record the number and kind of animals you find within the frame. You can also record information about the physical environment, such as the temperature, water depth, or size of soil particles. Decide if you want to include soil animals in your study, or just those on the surface. If you are working at the shore, you can extend your transect out into the water and find out what invertebrates inhabit the shallows.

Who Lives Where?

Measuring elevation

When you set up a transect on a beach or hillside, you can use a level and two yardsticks to figure out how much the ground slopes. Begin by holding one yardstick upright at the benchmark, and another at "+1." Stretch the transect line taut between the two sticks, and check to see that it is level. Read each yardstick where the transect line crosses it. Subtract the reading on the "+1" stick from that of the benchmark stick to determine the difference in elevation between the two. You will get a positive number when there is an **incline,** or uphill slope, and a negative number when there is a **decline,** or downhill slope. Move your yardsticks to the "+1" and "+2" positions, and continue until you have measured elevation along the entire length of the transect.

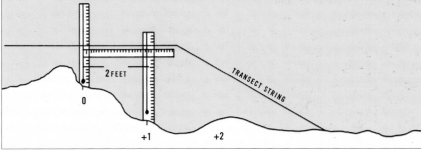

2 FEET

0

+1   +2

TRANSECT STRING

Using transect observations

Observing along a transect can help you learn about environmental variation and species distribution within a particular habitat. It can also help you compare different habitats.

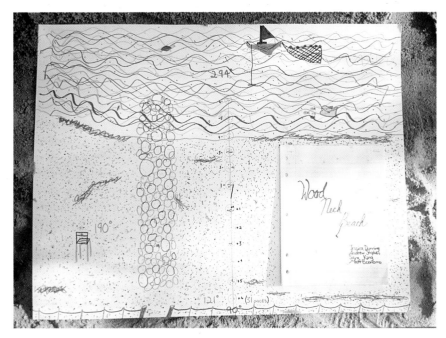

Investigations with Sponges

Many sponges have spicules with a characteristic shape. When scientists are trying to identify a particular kind of sponge, they often take a close look at its spicules. To see spicules, you must **isolate** them, or separate them from the rest of the sponge, and put them under a microscope.

Isolating spicules

Take a small piece of living sponge and put it in a bowl with a little water and some chlorine bleach. The bleach will cause the sponge cells to turn pale and break down, and the clear, glass-like spicules will collect on the bottom of the bowl. Remove some spicules and place them on a glass microscope slide. What do they look like?

SAFETY NOTE: Chlorine bleach is irritating to eyes and skin, and it takes the color out of fabric, so use it carefully.

Regeneration

If a small piece of a sponge is cut or broken off, it can often continue growing. The broken piece simply becomes a new individual. This type of reproduction is known as **regeneration**. Commercial sponge growers depend on this ability. They take "cuttings" from a sponge, attach them to concrete blocks, and put the blocks in water. After a few years, the sponges have grown large enough to be harvested and sold. If you are planning to maintain a saltwater aquarium over a long period of time, you can try growing a new, whole sponge from a cutting.

Regeneration is just one way that sponges reproduce. They can also develop **buds** that break off and continue growing. Some species release bunches of cells called **gemmules** into the water. These gemmules eventually release cells that develop into adult sponges. Sponges can also produce sperm and egg cells that join together and grow into new sponges. Most individual sponges are hermaphrodites, capable of producing both eggs and sperm.

Reaggregation experiment

Damaged sponges can sometimes continue growing through a process called **reaggregation**. If you want to observe this, take a small piece of living sponge and squeeze it through a piece of nylon stocking. This will destroy the structure of the sponge, but not the individual cells. Collect the cells in a glass bowl filled with fresh seawater. Aerate the water and keep track of how the sponge cells look. As weeks go by, cells might reaggregate, or clump together and grow into a new sponge.

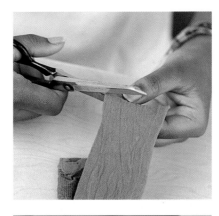

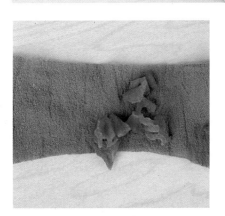

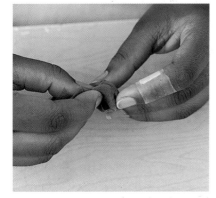

Setting up a Saltwater Aquarium

 saltwater aquarium can help you study the behavior of marine animals. It's easier to keep track of individual creatures in an aquarium than at the shore, and to observe them closely for long periods of time. Of course, an aquarium is a small, simple environment, and animals kept in one may behave differently than they would in their natural habitat. Combine aquarium-watching with frequent trips to the shore to help you draw more accurate conclusions about the behavior patterns of the animals in your tank.

Getting started

Before you collect any animals, decide if you have the space to set up an aquarium, and the time to maintain it. Talk over your plans with someone who has experience with saltwater tanks, or read up at the library. If you live along a coast, you will be able to collect local plants and animals for your aquarium, and release any that do not seem healthy. If you live inland, you will have the added expense of purchasing animals and chemicals for your tank from a pet store or supply company (see page 124). If you decide to set up an aquarium, gather the following equipment:

- A 10–30-gallon plastic or all-glass tank (metal seams can rust).
- Sturdy shelf, bench, or table to hold your tank.
- Filter with air pump. Under gravel filters, box filters, and pump circulating filters all work.
- Clean gravel or coarse sand. (If you are using an under gravel filter, make sure to get gravel that is larger than the holes in your filter, or the filter will clog.)
- Seawater, or a commercially

prepared salt mixture to make artificial seawater.
- You may need to buy an aquarium heater if you are keeping tropical animals, or a cooler if you are keeping cold-water animals in a warm building.

Setting up

1. Choose a permanent location for your tank. Once it is full you will not be able to move it. Choose a spot away from heaters and out of direct sunlight.
2. Wash your tank with water (no soap) and set it on the bench or table where you plan to keep it.
3. If you are using an under gravel filter, position it in the bottom of the tank.
4. Rinse gravel or sand several times. Put it in a bucket, cover it with water, then pour off the water.
5. Layer two inches of gravel on the bottom of the tank.
6. If you are using a box or pump circulating filter, set it up according to the manufacturer's directions. Connect any air hoses to the pump.

7. Cover the gravel with sheets of paper so it won't be stirred up when you add the water.
8. Fill your tank with seawater to within an inch of the top.
9. Turn on the pump to filter and aerate the water. Operate your tank for a couple of days before you add any animals so that the environment within your tank can stabilize.

Stocking your tank

After you are certain that your tank is working properly, you can collect or shop for animals to keep in it. Introduce just a few small animals at first. You can help animals adjust to the temperature of your tank by putting each in a small plastic bag with water from the place they were collected, and floating the bags in the tank for half an hour before releasing the animals. Keep an eye on your new animals for about a week. If they continue to look healthy, you can add a few more. Try not to overcrowd your tank. This leads to foul water and unhealthy animals, so be conservative when adding new specimens.

Small starfish, crabs, and sea urchins are hardy animals that do well in aquaria. Periwinkles and mud snails, barnacles, shrimp, and small fish are also good candidates.

Caring for aquarium animals

- Find out what, and how often, to feed the animals in your tank. Your own observations will inform you, as will books and other people who have studied marine animals. Many animals will eat small pieces of fish or squid, or brine shrimp you can raise from eggs purchased at a pet store or supply company. Add food in small amounts. Overfeeding will foul the water.
- Add fresh water to replace any lost by evaporation. If you are using chlorinated tap water, allow

it to sit overnight before putting it in the tank. Don't add seawater! When water evaporates from your tank, the salts are left behind. Adding seawater will make your tank more and more salty.
- Scoop out about a quarter of the water in the aquarium once a month, and replace it with fresh seawater.
- If you have a box or outside filter, replace the glass wool when it becomes dirty.
- If algae grows on the inside of the glass, you can scrape it off with a special tool designed for this purpose, and available at a pet store or supply company.

75

THE ROCKY SHORE

Rocky shores are great places to find marine plants and animals. Unlike shifting sand, rocks provide a firm base that organisms can cling to when waves wash over them. Organisms that attach themselves to rocks can maintain their position

relative to the sun, a food supply, or potential mates. Schedule a trip to a rocky shore at low tide so you can explore as much of the intertidal zone as possible.

Where to look

Search through seaweeds for marine animals and their eggs. Attached seaweeds provide animals with food and shelter.

Gently turn over rocks to see if any animals are underneath. Rocks offer protection from predators, waves, and sun. Always replace rocks the way you found them, so the animals that live on and under them are not injured or disturbed.

Cracks, crevices, and shady spots underneath large rocks are good places to look.

Tide pools are places that remain full of water even when the tide goes out and leaves nearby areas high and dry. Starfish, sea anemones, crabs, and many other animals inhabit tide pools.

Wade out into shallow water if it is safe to do so. What plants and animals can you find there? What organisms live on the exposed rocks nearby?

It's a hard-knock life

Wind, rain, and pounding waves all beat against the rocky shore. They threaten to wash away the organisms that make their home in this environment. But many plants and animals have ways of holding on to the rocks.

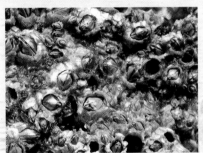

▶ Adult barnacles live inside a case that looks like a little volcano. The case is permanently stuck to the rocks with a special cement made by the barnacle. If you want to see just how strong this cement is, find the empty case of a barnacle that has died, and try to pry it off!

▶ Periwinkles, limpets, and other snail-like animals cling to the rocks with a soft, slimy "foot." They move around on, as well as hang on with, this muscular foot.

▶ A structure called a **holdfast** keeps seaweeds attached to rocks. Some holdfasts look like little suction cups. Others look like gnarly, tangled roots.

A mussel's **byssal threads** anchor it to the rocks. These threads are secreted by a special gland on the mussel's body. Newly secreted byssal threads are liquid, but they soon harden in the water.

▶ The **tube feet** on a starfish help it cling to rocks and shells.

The operculum, or door, is easy to see on the shell of this Atlantic dogwinkle, Thais lapillus. T. lapillus *preys on mussels and barnacles.*

Safety Notes

▶ Explore with a partner.

▶ Wear boots, old sneakers, or "reef shoes" when you visit a rocky shore. They'll keep your feet from being cut by barnacles, sharp rocks, and broken glass.

▶ Remember that seaweed-covered rocks are more slippery than they look!

▶ In places where rocks drop steeply into deep water or get pounded by large waves, stay well back from the water's edge.

▶ Always keep track of the tide. In some places the water level rises quickly once the tide has turned!

Pressing Seaweed

aking your own seaweed collection is a great way to learn to recognize different species. You can preserve seaweed by drying and flattening it in a plant press. A collection of mounted, pressed plant specimens is called a **herbarium.** Herbariums are used by marine biologists and botanists.

These two pressed seaweeds are specimens of the red alga called dulce, Rhodomenia palmata. *In parts of Canada, Scotland, and Ireland, dulce is harvested, dried, and eaten as a snack food.*

Setting up

To start your herbarium you will need:

- Seaweed.
- Heavy white paper that will not tear when wet. (Try oaktag, heavy drawing paper, or index cards, or order herbarium paper from one of the biological supply companies listed on page 124.)
- Cake pan or large, shallow plastic container.
- Water.
- Fine-weave white cloth (pieces of an old sheet will do).
- Lots of newspaper.
- Plant press (available from supply companies) or a board with bricks or rocks to weight it.
- White glue, glue stick, or paste.
- Field guide or illustrated book about seaweeds.

Directions

▶ Collect a few seaweeds. Keep them cool and moist in a pan of cold water until you are ready to press them.

▶ Put a piece of heavy white paper in the bottom of your pan, and cover it with a thin layer of water.

▶ Float a piece of seaweed above the paper. Arrange it so its shape is clearly visible.

▶ Trim the seaweed if it is too large for your paper, or if it has many overlapping "branches."

▶ Gently remove the paper from the pan of water, taking care to keep the seaweed in place.

► Cover the seaweed with a piece of cloth.

► Put the mounted, cloth-covered seaweed between thick layers of newspaper. The cloth will insure that your specimen sticks to the mounting paper below it, but not to the newspaper above.

► Repeat this procedure with other seaweeds, until you have mounted all the specimens you want to press.

► Stack all your specimens and layers of newspaper in your plant press and tighten the strap that holds it together, or simply put a board weighted with bricks or stones on top of your stack.

► Replace the newspapers with dry ones twice a day.

► After a week or so, the cloth and white paper surrounding your specimens will feel quite dry. Throw out the newspapers and peel back the cloth. Most of your specimens will be stuck to the mounting paper by the slippery substance that coated the fresh seaweeds. If one comes loose, glue it back with white glue diluted with water, a glue stick, or paste.

► Label each specimen with your name and the date and place where you collected it. A field guide or book about marine algae will help you identify and name unfamiliar specimens.

► Store your specimens flat on a shelf, in a box, or in a paper folder. If they start to curl up, put them back in your plant press for a few days.

Notes about collecting

Seaweeds provide many marine animals with food, shelter, and places to lay their eggs. People count on seaweeds, too. We use them for food, and in the manufacture of drugs, cosmetics, and many other products. Marine plants are important plants to have around, so practice the following conservation rules when you collect:

• Collect just a few specimens at a time. When you have pressed them, you can go back for more if you need to. It's easy to gather much more seaweed than you can deal with!

• Only collect a specimen if you can find others like it growing nearby. Many seaweeds you will find are common, but some are rare in certain areas, and should be left where they are.

• When you leave a collecting spot, leave it as you found it. Replace any rocks you have turned over or removed, so you don't disrupt the living conditions of marine life there.

• When collecting, take note of your environment. Describe where you find each specimen, and what it is growing on. If you can, figure out whether it is from a place that is always covered by water, or one that is exposed at low tide. Sketch or list any animals or eggs you find on a specimen and other nearby plants. You may want to record each plant's color, since pressed seaweed often fades. Your field notes will help you learn and remember a lot about the

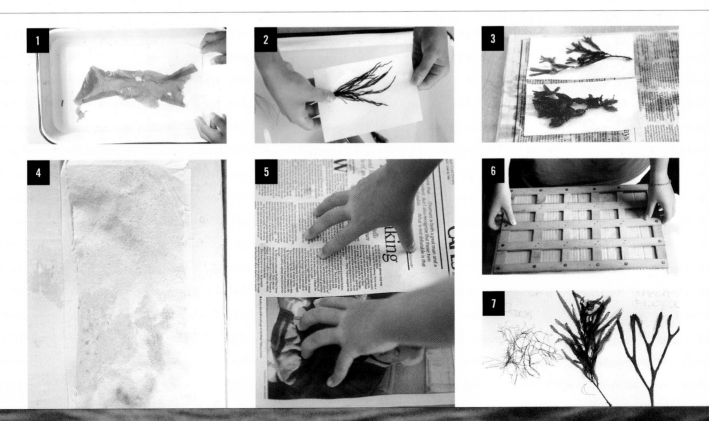

Fish

The next time you go fishing, plan to take a close look at your catch before you clean and cook it. Or buy a fish at a grocery store or fish market to study.

Fish are adapted for life in a very different environment than ours, and it's interesting to see the ways their bodies are like, and unlike, our own.

Scientists recognize three large groups of fish. Lampreys and other jawless fish belong to the class Agnatha. The Chondrichthyes, or sharks and rays, have a skeleton made of cartilage (the same tissue that makes up your ear) instead of bone. Trout, bass, tuna, and most of the species we use for food belong to the Osteichthyes, the class of bony fishes.

A close look at a bony fish

The shape of a fish's body will tell you something about the way it lives.

A streamlined body helps a fish swim fast, while a flattened shape is good for crawling or hiding along the ocean bottom. Long, snake-like fish easily slip through weeds, into holes, and in between rocks.

A fish's fins help it move through the water. They also stabilize the fish so it doesn't tip over as it swims. Fins can have other functions as well. There are fish that use their fins to find food, cling to rocks, signal to other fish, and attract mates. Some fins are paired, others are single, and each has a special

CAUDAL FIN

DORSAL FIN

PECTORAL FIN

ANAL FIN

Bony spines support the dorsal fin of this scup. These spines are movable, as are the softer, more flexible rays in some of the scup's other fins. Spines and rays allow fish to open and close their fins, or ripple them.

name. The **dorsal fin** is on a fish's back, and the **caudal fin** is on its tail. Each kind of fish uses its fins in particular ways. The barracuda, a fast swimmer, uses its strong body and large caudal fin to propel itself through the water. Its small dorsal fin provides stability. The sea horse swims with a rippling movement of its dorsal fin. It has a **prehensile** tail without a caudal fin, which it uses to grab hold of aquatic plants. Watching live fish in aquaria is a good way to see how fins work.

The side-to-side movements of this fish's body are largely responsible for driving it forward, but its caudal fin also pushes against the water.

Some fish have **scales** that protect their skin from injury and infection. Other fish have skin that is coated with slimy **mucus**.

Scientists can often tell how old a fish is by counting the growth rings, or annuli, on its scales.

Fish see with their eyes, as we do. They have no eyelids, so their eyes never close, but a layer of clear skin protects their eyes. Fish can also smell, but unlike us, they smell underwater. The **nares** in a fish's snout are like our nostrils. They lead to a pouch inside the snout lined with special cells that are sensitive to chemicals in the water. Many fish use their sense of smell to locate food. Others rely on it to direct them when they migrate.

Fish have another sensory system called the **lateral line**. Since human beings don't have anything

quite like it, it's difficult for us to understand just how it works. The lateral line is a system of canals, nerves, and special cells called **neuromasts** that can detect tiny movements in the water. Scientists think the lateral line system helps fish sense the movements of other animals in the water, alerting them to nearby predators or food. It may also pick up information about water currents.

Fish need oxygen just like we do, and their **gills** extract it from the water. All bony fish have five gills on each side of their head. These important and delicate structures are protected by a gill cover called the operculum. Some fish also get oxygen through the skin lining their mouth, or through lungs.

The thin, dark line on the side of this scup is part of its lateral line system.

Fish Prints

Printing is one way to record the shape, size, and appearance of a fish. It is also a fun way to create beautiful pictures and clothing. The materials you will need are inexpensive and easy to find.

Materials

- Newspaper.
- A whole fish (one you've caught, or bought at a fish market).
- Rags or paper towels.
- Acrylic paint or water-base printing ink.*
- Tray, or pane of glass with taped edges.
- Brayer* or paint brush.
- Paper, cloth, or T-shirt to print on.

Directions

▶ Cover your work space with a layer of old newspaper.

▶ Rinse your fish in water, then blot it dry with a rag or paper towel.

▶ Squeeze a small amount of paint or ink onto the tray or glass.

▶ Roll the brayer in the ink to coat it, or dip a paint brush into the ink.

▶ Ink one side of your fish with the brayer or paint brush. A thin, even layer of paint or ink makes the best print.

▶ Put the fish, ink side down, on a piece of paper, fabric, or T-shirt.

▶ Gently press down on the fish with your fingers. Try to press each part of it, especially fins and other parts that curve away from the paper or fabric.

▶ Remove the fish by lifting it straight up.

▶ When your print is dry, you can add colored markings or other details with a paint brush or pen.

* ACRYLIC PAINT, INK, AND BRAYERS ARE AVAILABLE AT ART SUPPLY STORES. IF YOU ARE PRINTING ON FABRIC, MAKE SURE TO USE ACRYLIC PAINT OR A PRINTING INK THAT WILL NOT WASH OUT WHEN THE FABRIC IS WASHED.

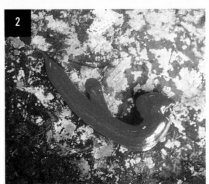

Try adding seaweed prints to your fish designs for another great look. Remember to blot seaweed dry before applying paint or ink.

Bugs, Bugs, Bugs

From the bees that provide us with honey and wax to the cockroaches that share our crumbs, insects amaze us, pester us, and help us to survive. Scientists have described and studied close to one million different species of insects. This makes them the largest **class** of animals on earth, larger than all the other groups combined! Indoors and outside, insects are wherever you go; they live in nearly every place on Earth and in just about every environment. With so many different species in so many sizes, shapes, and colors, how can you tell when you're actually looking at an authentic insect? Here are a few things that just about all insects share and that you can look for:

- Segmented bodies: All insects have bodies made up of many small sections called **segments**. The segments are lined up in a row and are usually grouped into three larger divisions: the **head**, the **thorax**, and the **abdomen**. The insect's mouth, eyes, and antennae are found on the head, while its legs and wings grow from the thorax, the middle section.
- Exoskeletons: All insects have a tough outer skin called the **exoskeleton**, which protects their soft inner organs and gives them their shape.
- Jointed legs: All insects have three pairs of jointed legs. Other animals that seem like insects but have more, like spiders, are not true insects.

The scientists who study insects are called **entomologists**, and the projects in this chapter will get you started on being an entomologist yourself! You'll raise caterpillars (p. 90) and milkweed bugs (p. 94) to study their life cycles and behavior, and you'll learn how to collect insects outdoors and preserve and mount them in your own collection (p. 100). You'll also learn how to identify many different kinds of insects with a field guide (p. 102).

GETTING STARTED

T

he best way to learn about insects is to find one and watch it. What does it look like? How does it move? What does it do? These are questions you can answer yourself by looking.

In the field

Fields are home to many insects. When you visit a field, carefully search the stems, leaves, and flowers of plants. You'll find bees and butterflies collecting nectar, beetles and caterpillars munching on leaves, and bugs sucking the juice out of plant stems. Look overhead. You may see dragonflies scouting for prey. Check under rocks for beetle larvae and ant nests. Listen for insects. Grasshoppers and crickets may be easier to hear than to see. Look for signs of insects, too. Some leave traces that let you know where they have been.

A garden trowel may aid your search for soil-dwelling insects.

A notebook or sketch pad and pencil will help you record and remember what you see.

Equipment

A few simple tools will help you study many different kinds of insects.

A hand lens, or magnifying glass, will help you get a more detailed look at the insects you find.

A net can help you catch insects that tend to fly away before you can study them.

An empty coffee can, jar, or clear plastic container temporarily holds an insect you may want to watch.

Using a Net

One way to use a net is to sweep it through tall stands of grass or wildflowers using short, quick strokes. Many insects will end up in the net, even though only a few were visible beforehand. Sometimes it's possible to net an insect in flight. Either way, by turning the net handle you can close the opening to prevent the insects from escaping. Look through the mesh net to see what you have caught, or gently transfer them to a container for further study. Most insects, even stinging ones, can be handled safely if you are careful. Of course, if you are allergic to bees you must avoid handling them.

Noticing changes

Return often to the same place to look for insects. Populations can change dramatically over time. Insects that are difficult to find during one visit may be common later on. Particular behavior, like courtship or egg laying, may give way to new activity. What changes in a familiar place can you notice over time?

Insect Orders

T he class **Insecta** includes a large and diverse group of animals. Scientists divide these animals into twenty-five to thirty orders. Learning the characteristics of all of these orders is a difficult task. To begin, focus on the orders that include familiar insects.

Twelve common orders are described here. As you read, think if you have ever seen an insect that fits each description. Classifying the insects you already know will help you to understand taxonomy.

An introduction to some orders of insects

The **Odonata** are dragonflies and damselflies. Adults have two pairs of large, veined wings, large eyes, and long, slender abdomens. Odonate nymphs are **aquatic,** and undergo gradual metamorphosis. The name

Odonata means "tooth." Though odonates don't have actual teeth, they are impressive hunters.

Crickets, grasshoppers, locusts, praying mantids, and cockroaches make up the order **Orthoptera,**

which means "straight wings." Many insects in this order have four wings; others have two or none.

They have chewing mouthparts, and metamorphosis is gradual. The males of many species are known for the chirping sounds they make to attract mates.

Termites belong to the order **Isoptera.** These insects live in colonies in the ground or in wood, have chewing mouthparts, and gradual metamorphosis. Because some species of termites colonize houses and other wood-frame buildings, chewing away at the structural elements, termites are well known to many people.

The **Dermaptera,** or earwigs, are crawling insects. Most have a pair of short, thick wings with another pair folded underneath. Dermaptera means "skin wing" and refers to the leathery front wings. The common name comes from a false belief that these insects crawl into people's ears. Earwigs have chewing mouthparts, pincer-like **cerci,** and gradual metamorphosis.

The **Anoplura** are tiny wingless insects with sucking mouthparts. They are parasites of mammals. This group includes the head lice and body lice that parasitize humans. Metamorphosis is gradual.

The **Hemiptera,** or "half wings," are aquatic and **terrestrial.** Adult bugs usually have two pairs of wings. The hind wings are membranous, and the forewings are leathery near the body and membranous away from it. When a bug is not using its wings to fly, they are folded over its body with the tips overlapping.

This creates an "X" pattern on the insect's back. Hemiptera have sucking mouthparts. Some bugs feed on plant juices, while others prey on animals. Metamorphosis is gradual.

Cicadas, leafhoppers, and aphids are some of the insects that make up the order **Homoptera**. Like the Hemiptera, they undergo gradual metamorphosis and their mouthparts are adapted for piercing and sucking. Some lack wings, while others have wings that are held in a  roof-like or tent-like fashion over their bodies when not in use. All feed on plants.

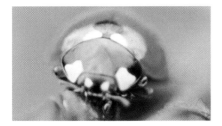

The **Coleoptera**, or "sheath-winged" insects, are the beetles. The forewings, or **elytra**, of adult beetles usually meet in the middle  of the back and cover the hind wings, forming a line or "T" pattern. Beetles undergo complete metamorphosis, with larvae that look a little like

caterpillars with hard, shiny heads. Larvae are sometimes referred to as "grubs." Both adults and larvae have chewing mouthparts. There are more species of beetles than of any other insect order.

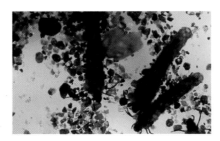

The **Trichoptera,** or caddisflies, are bound to be encountered by anyone who explores streams, lakes, or ponds. Adult caddisflies, or "Dusty Millers," look something like moths, with their wings held tent-like over their bodies. Trichoptera undergo complete metamorphosis, and larvae are aquatic. Most species construct individual homes, or cases, out of bits of vegetation, small stones, or sand grains. They drag their homes with them wherever they go.

The **Lepidoptera** include the butterflies and moths. Adults typically have four wings that are covered with tiny scales, hence the name Lepidoptera, or "scaly wings." Most adults have a long, coiled proboscis that is used to suck nectar or other liquid food. Metamorphosis is complete, and larvae, or caterpillars, have chewing mouthparts. They pupate in a chrysalis or cocoon, depending on the species.

Flies, mosquitoes, and gnats belong to the order **Diptera**. These insects have just one pair of wings, hence the name Diptera, or "two-wings." Complete metamorphosis is characteristic of this order, and larvae may be terrestrial or aquatic. Adults have sucking mouthparts, as anyone who has been bitten by a mosquito will recall.

Bees, wasps, and ants belong to the order **Hymenoptera**. The name of this order translates as "membrane-winged;" two pairs of thin, clear, membranous wings are characteristic of these insects during some phase of their life cycle. All adult bees and wasps have wings. In ants, only those that are about to mate have wings. The workers and soldiers we commonly see climbing in and out of ant hills lack them. Many female hymenoptera have a stinger or an egg-laying organ at the end of their abdomens. These insects undergo complete metamorphosis. Many hymenoptera are **social insects,** living together in colonies.

Raising Caterpillars

A ny caterpillar or larva you find in the field will grow into a butterfly or moth. Caterpillars can be kept in fish tanks or large glass jars. Wire screening or cheesecloth over the top will allow fresh air to circulate. The top should be securely fastened so the caterpillars don't escape and end up where they can't find food and water. Some stores sell large plastic boxes specially designed as "bug houses" that can be used to house a caterpillar. Caterpillar cages can also be made by shaping wire screening into a cylinder, fastening it, and adding two aluminum cake pans for the top and the bottom. Cut white paper or oaktag to fit the bottom of the cage. Insects are often easier to see against a light background.

Food

Caterpillars in captivity need plenty of fresh food; many eat at an astonishing rate. Some caterpillars are picky eaters. Monarch larvae eat only milkweed. Black swallowtail larvae feed on parsley, carrots, and related plants. Gypsy moth larvae are less particular. They seem to prefer oak leaves, but find maple, birch, beech, and cherry digestible as well. In a pinch, they'll even eat pine needles!

Take note of a caterpillar's natural surroundings before you collect it; it may be chewing away on the very plant it requires for food. If you want to keep a caterpillar that does not seem to be on its food plant, a field guide or other reference book may help you determine what it eats. If you are still unsure, it is best to release the caterpillar where you

found it once you have finished observing it. Simply filling its cage with grass or leaves may not be enough to keep your caterpillars healthy, since not all caterpillars can make use of these "foods."

Care

Keep a caterpillar's cage clean, stocked with food, and out of direct sunlight. Remove any wilted leaves or other uneaten food each day, and periodically empty feces from the bottom of the cage. Most caterpillars get water from the food they eat; you do not need to supply a bottle or dish for drinking. A few drops of water sprinkled on a leaf can be helpful, but guard against too much moisture. Dumping in a lot of damp leaves, or failing to remove old food, can create a moldy, unhealthy environment in the cage.

Time to pupate

Sooner or later your caterpillar will stop eating and be ready to pupate. It might form a chrysalis right on its food plant, as monarch caterpillars do, or spin a cocoon on a leaf or

© BILL IVY

on the side of the cage. Some caterpillars tunnel into the soil and pupate underground. Add two or three inches of moist soil to the bottom of your cage if you are raising a tunneling species. A field

guide may help you determine the needs of your particular caterpillar. If not, release it outside to pupate.

Overwintering

Some butterflies and moths have a short pupal stage and you will see adults emerge in a few weeks. When their wings are dry, let them go. Other species **overwinter** as pupae and won't emerge until spring. Keep overwintering pupae in a cool place. If there is soil in your container, check it regularly to make sure it stays a bit damp. When the weather begins to get warm, check your container daily and release any newly emerged adults.

Dragonflies and Damselflies

Dragonflies and damselflies spend the first part of their lives as nymphs, underwater. You may find them crawling on aquatic plants, or in the silt and decaying vegetation on the bottom of a pond or stream. Watch for adults resting on plants or flying above the water.

Which is which?

It is easy to tell damselfly and dragonfly nymphs apart. A damselfly nymph has a long, slender body with three tail-like **gills** that allow it to "breathe" underwater. It moves through the water by wriggling from side to side. A dragonfly nymph looks more sturdy. It has a much wider abdomen with a special **gill chamber** inside. Dragonflies move, as well as breathe, by pumping water in and out of this chamber.

You can recognize adult damselflies by their thin, delicate bodies, and by their wings. Both pairs of wings are similar in size and shape, and the damselflies tend to tip them up or fold them parallel to their bodies when resting. Dragonflies are stockier, and their hind wings are wider near the abdomen than their forewings are. Dragonflies usually hold their wings out horizontally when they are not flying.

Though it is easy to tell damselflies from dragonflies, identifying different kinds within each group can be quite difficult. In some species, adult males and females are different colors. An individual's color can change over time as well. A breeding male may be much brighter than a young or aging one. Identifying nymphs can be even harder than identifying adults. In fact, many species of odonates are known only from adult specimens; scientists are not sure what the nymphs look like! Sometimes entomologists have to raise a nymph to adulthood in order to identify it.

Metamorphosis

An odonate nymph molts many times underwater. When it is ready for its final molt, it crawls up a plant stem, or rock, or onto shore until

its entire body is out of the water. Its skin splits, and the adult crawls out, unfolding a surprisingly long abdomen and wings. The newly emerged adult is called an **imago**. When its wings are dry and its body is hard, it will fly off in search of food.

Life in the air

Dragonflies and damselflies live just a few weeks as airborne adults. During this time you can watch them hunt, patrol their territories, court, mate, and lay eggs. Female odonates deposit their eggs in water. Some fly above the surface, dipping their abdomens down into the water and releasing eggs as they go. Others lay eggs on aquatic plants, or in the sand or mud near shore. Adult odonates have huge eyes, which help them locate flying insects to eat. They snatch their prey out of the air with their long legs, which form a kind of basket when they fly.

Rearing damselflies and dragonflies

Nymphs from still water are easy to raise as long as you provide them with plenty of food! Keep them in aquaria or shallow pans with a layer of sand, gravel, or pond muck on the bottom. Replace evaporated water with pond or spring water rather than tap water, as the chemicals in tap water may harm aquatic animals. You can collect small crustacea and insects from a pond for them to eat. Lean a stick against the side of the container, or roll a strip of gauze or cheesecloth down into the water so the nymphs can crawl out when it is time for their metamorphosis to adulthood.

Most odonate nymphs live underwater for about a year, though some damselfly species mature in just a few months. Large dragonflies may take three or four years.

93

Damselflies mating

Taxonomy

ORDER: *Odonata (dragonflies and damselflies)*
SUBORDERS: *Anisoptera (dragonflies) Zygoptera (damselflies)*
FAMILIES: *Petaluridae Agrionidae, Gomphidae, Coenagrionidae, Aeschnidae, Corduligasteridae, Libellulidae*

Raising Milkweed Bugs

Raising milkweed bugs will give you a chance to observe the life cycle of an insect with gradual metamorphosis. Milkweed bugs belong to the family Lygeidae, or seed bugs.

Finding milkweed bugs

If you live in an area where milkweed plants are common, you will probably be able to find milkweed bugs. The large milkweed bug, *Oncopeltus fasciatus*, reaches a length of about one-half inch. You may also find the small milkweed bug, *Lygaeus kalmii*. Milkweed

Look through a hand lens to get a close-up view of milkweed bugs.

bugs thrive in warm weather, and in some places you can find adults year round. In northern areas many nymphs and adults die when cold weather hits, and some adults migrate south. Although a new generation will return north the following summer, you may not start finding them until mid-season.

You can find adults and nymphs crawling among milkweed flowers and on the underside of leaves. You may also find them on the ground at the base of the milkweed plant, for if they were disturbed by your approach, they may drop to the ground to keep out of harm's way. You may even find milkweed bug eggs, which are laid in clusters of fifteen to thirty under leaves or between pods.

Mail order bugs

If you live in an area where milkweed is not common, or if you want to raise milkweed bugs at a time of year when they cannot be found outdoors, you can order some from a biological supply company (see page 124). Supply companies collect or raise organisms that interest students and researchers, and for a few dollars you can have milkweed bugs delivered to your door. Milkweed bugs obtained from a supply house are easier to maintain than wild ones, for they have been bred to feed on sunflower seeds instead of milkweed pods.

REMEMBER: If you live in an area where milkweed bugs are not native, you will need to freeze any insects and eggs that are alive when you have finished studying them. Releasing insects outdoors in an area where they do not ordinarily live can cause trouble. They might fail to find food and starve to death. Or more problematically, they might thrive and reproduce overwhelmingly, unchecked by native predators.

Housing and feeding your bugs

Keep your milkweed bugs in a clean, dry container. A one-gallon glass jar, a small aquarium, or a cage made with wire screening will do. Wild bugs need to be supplied with milkweed pods containing seeds. Nymphs will feed on flowers as well. Mail order bugs can be given hulled, unsalted sunflower seeds. A small vial of water plugged with cotton or a piece of damp sponge will provide enough water for your bugs. Of course, your container will need a bug-proof lid. Cheesecloth and screening both work well. Make

Place a cotton ball or piece of cloth inside a small jar, lid, or cup and put it in your container. This will make a milkweed leaf substitute for the females to lay eggs on. If your container becomes crowded with bugs, move the eggs to a new jar. A single female may lay as many as two thousand eggs in her lifetime, and overcrowding can lead to cannibalism.

They will molt five times before they are fully grown. The stage between each molt is called an instar. Observing the shed exoskeletons as well as the actual nymphs will help you to understand what changes occur between instars.

sure that fresh food and water are always available. Since bugs feed by sucking the contents of a seed and leaving the outside, you will need to remove the shrunken seed casings that are left behind.

What can you notice?

Adult milkweed bugs live for thirty to forty days. During that time they mate, and females lay eggs. You can tell adult males from females by the color pattern on the **ventral**, or under, side of their abdomens.

Males have two black bands separated by a plain band of orange. In females, the orange band has a black spot on each side.

Eggs hatch in about four days. Newly hatched nymphs are tiny— as small as the head of a pin!

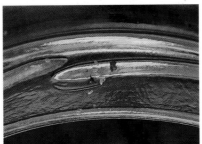

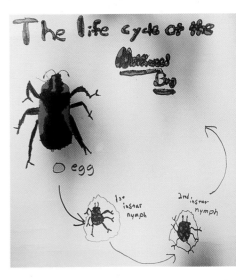

Taxonomy

ORDER: Hemiptera (bugs)
FAMILY: Lygeidae (seed bugs)
GENUS AND SPECIES: Oncopeltus fasciatus (the large milkweed bug), Lygaeus kalmii (the small milkweed bug)

Galls

Galls are abnormal growths on plants. They are evidence of another fascinating relationship between insects and plants. Many kinds of galls are caused (or **induced**) by insects. A gall is formed when a female insect lays an egg on or in a plant. She may also deposit a chemical on the plant. This chemical, or the secretions or feeding activity of the newly hatched larva, makes the plant grow in an unusual way. The swelling plant tissue surrounds the developing larva, providing it with food and shelter.

How to find galls

You can hunt for galls wherever there are plants. Look for unusual spots or swellings on leaves, twigs, and stems. Goldenrod flowers and oak trees are especially good plants to search because they tend to have more galls than many other species. Scientists aren't sure why.

Once you start looking for galls, you will discover many different kinds. Gall-inducing insects are particular about the plants they lay their eggs on, and each species of insect causes a specific type of gall.

Noting what the gall looks like and identifying the plant it is on will help you determine what kind of insect induced it, even if the insect itself has matured and left.

Goldenrod galls

Goldenrod ball galls are induced by *Eurosta solidaginis*, a fruit fly.

Fly larvae spend the winter inside ball galls, then pupate and emerge as adults in the spring. Elliptical goldenrod galls have small caterpillars inside. Eventually, they emerge as moths. Blister galls look like black spots on goldenrod leaves. They are caused by a type of midge (an insect in the order Diptera).

Oak apples

Hundreds of different kinds of galls can be found on oak trees. Oak apple galls, which grow on twigs and leaves, are some of the more obvious. They are light brown or tan, and can be an inch or two in diameter. Tiny wasp larvae live at the center, surrounded by hair-like fibers that radiate outward. There are many kinds of oak apples, each caused by a different species of wasp in the family Cynipidae.

Common and confounding

Galls are common, but entomologists still have a lot to learn about the insects that cause them. Most gall makers are tiny. As larvae they are hidden inside plants, and as adults they can be hard to find. This makes them both fascinating and difficult to study! There are about fifteen hundred species of insects in North America that induce galls. Certain mites, nematode worms, bacteria, and fungi can induce galls as well.

Anybody home?

If you carefully search the surface of a gall, you may find tiny **exit holes** where the inhabitant chewed its way out of its former home. Large holes in the gall are apt to be the work of another animal; downy woodpeckers, red squirrels, and certain species of mice have learned to search out galls in order to eat the larvae inside. Small spiders and insects may move into a gall if the original inhabitant gets eaten or moves on.

Galls without exit holes may still harbor the inducing insect, but sometimes they hold surprises. New insects may move in alongside the original larvae, or parasitic insects may lay their eggs within the gall. When parasite larvae hatch, they feed upon the gall maker.

97

Gall-Watching

If you want to see what emerges from a gall, you can dig up the entire plant it is on and pot it indoors. You can also leave the gall where you find it, but cover it with a bag sewn of flexible tent screening so the emerging insect can't fly away until you've had a look at it. Some host plants die or enter a **dormant** period in the fall. When they do, you can collect some of their galls and keep them indoors in a shoebox or empty jar until the insects inside tunnel out. Be prepared to be patient! Some larvae eat and grow inside a gall all summer, pupate over the winter, and emerge as adults the following spring.

EXPLORING THE

Y ou don't have to go far to find interesting insects to study. You don't even have to set foot outdoors. House crickets, fruit flies, cockroaches, and clothes moths often share people's homes. So do fleas, flies, and carpenter ants. Some insects, like mosquitoes, are just passing through. Others, like termites, usually move in for good. Go inside and take a good look around. What insects live with you?

Flies, carpenter ants, and termites are insects you might find sharing your home.

©BILL IVY

©BILL IVY

©BILL IVY

Cockroaches

©BILL IVY

There are thousands of species of cock-roaches in the world. If you live in a city, chances are you will be able to find *Blatella germanica*, the German cockroach, without looking hard at all. These insects live in all kinds of buildings: apartments, stores, schools, subway stations, museums, and restaurants. Domestic cockroaches are perfectly adapted for life among people. Their flattened bodies fit easily into tiny cracks in walls or spaces under objects. They are fast runners, with nervous systems that enable them to get moving almost as soon as they perceive danger. Long, sensitive antennae and cerci collect information about their surroundings, helping them to find food and water, and avoid danger. Finding food is rarely a problem. *B. germanica* can eat any food crumbs or scraps of food we happen to leave out for them.

If we clean up carefully after every meal, they can make do with cat food left out in a dish, insulation, the glue on wallpaper, stamps, and bookbindings, whatever is handy. They can even do without food and water for weeks at a time. As insects go, domestic cockroaches appear to be fairly intelligent. In laboratories, they have learned to run mazes and avoid areas sprayed with particular insecticides.

Other cockroaches, like the woodroach, are usually found outside. Outdoor roaches tend to spend their days in moist places: under stones, plants, logs, or among fallen leaves. Like indoor roaches, they are most active at night, and find places to hide during the day. Water pipes, kitchens, bathrooms, and other damp places often attract indoor roaches. Cockroaches are ancient animals. Fossils as old as 250 million years have been found that look quite similar to today's species. Apparently, cockroaches were as well suited to life among dinosaurs as they are to life among people.

GREAT INDOORS

Window lights and street lights

Some insects are attracted to light, and will fly to lighted windows at night. You can easily observe them from inside, or you can take a flashlight and go out. You may discover many species that are new to you crawling across your screens on a summer evening. Check porch lights and streetlamps, too. Moths, beetles, and other insects are often drawn to them. Insects that have accidentally ended up inside a building may fly at windows during the day in search of a way back out.

Making a Collection

 aking a collection can help you learn more about insect anatomy, identification, and classification. You may want to collect a variety of insects, or just one species.

Equipment

Before you start collecting insects, assemble the following equipment. It will help you with your work.

A **net** can help you catch insects that are difficult to capture with your bare hands.

A **killing can** is used to contain and kill insects. Coffee cans with plastic lids work well.

Pins are used to mount many insects. Use special insect pins rather than sewing pins, which may rust or be too thick for some delicate insects. Pins come in many sizes: 0, 1, 2, and 3 will be most useful. You can order them from one of the supply houses listed on page 124.

Boxes with cork or foam lining the bottom are used to mount and store specimens. You can adapt a cigar box, but boxes specifically designed for collectors are easiest to use. They are available from biological supply houses.

How to kill insects

Some entomologists use poisons to kill insects, but a much safer method also works. Simply leave the insects in a covered can and put the can in a freezer for a few hours. Once the insects are dead, let them thaw out before you handle them.

Conservation

Be selective when you collect. Here are some guidelines:
- ▶ Collect only one specimen of any species, unless it is considered a **pest**.
- ▶ Collect all the pests you want, such as Japanese beetles, gypsy moths, and cabbage-white butterflies.
- ▶ Collect only adult insects. Leave larvae and nymphs. Most larvae and nymphs require special preservation techniques.
- ▶ Collect insects that are already dead.
- ▶ Release insects that help control pests, such as praying mantids and ladybeetles.
- ▶ Release insects that are rare, or uncommon to your particular collecting site.

This Japanese beetle is considered a pest; collect as many as you want.

Collecting

You can pick insects up with your fingers, or catch them with a net. To transfer them to your killing can, hold the tip of your net straight up so that the insects will work their way up into it. Then gently invert the end of the net into your open can. It takes practice to learn to do this successfully; you may lose some insects in the beginning. Observe and then release insects that you do not plan to add to your collection.

Field notes

Make sure to record the date and location where you collect a specimen. You can also make field notes about its behavior or appearance.

Pinning

Many insects can be pinned directly into storage and display boxes.

Choose the pin size that is appropriate for each specimen. Beetles and leafhoppers are usually pinned through the right wing, bugs are pinned above the "X" formed by the crossed forewings, and flies and grasshoppers are pinned through the right part of the thorax. Some insects are so small that even the finest of pins are too large for them. These insects can be fixed to a small triangle of stiff paper with a dot of glue. The pin can be put through the paper instead of directly through the insect. Make sure to pin insects soon after they are killed so that they don't become brittle. You can keep them in an airtight

box in the freezer if there will be several days between collecting and pinning. If specimens become too brittle to work with, they can be relaxed by putting them in a jar with a damp piece of blotting paper or a few drops of water on the bottom.

Spreading

Butterflies, dragonflies, grasshoppers, and many other insects are often displayed with one or both pairs of wings open. **Spreading boards** are used to prepare these specimens. First, position the insect with its body in the center groove of the spreading board. Pin strips of paper over the wings. Remove one pin and gently position the wing nearest it with a tweezers. Replace the pin, and continue until all wings are positioned. Leave the insect on the board until it is completely dry. This may take a few days or as long as two weeks.

Labeling

Two labels made of heavy paper are usually pinned underneath each insect in a collection. The first identifies the insect and lists the date and place it was captured. The collector's name is put on a second label.

Protecting your collection

Store your collection in a dry place. Make sure that the box lid fits tightly. Dermestid beetles will eat dried insects, among other things, and a tight lid will discourage them from making a meal of your collection. Some collectors add mothballs or flakes to their boxes to keep dermestids away.

Identifying Insects

Identifying insects means recognizing the details of behavior or appearance that distinguish one type of insect from another. Identification can occur at many levels. Sometimes you simply want to know if the animal you are observing is an insect or another kind of arthropod.

Is it a beetle or a bug?

Often, you know you have found an insect but aren't sure whether to call it a beetle or a bug. With experience you will be able to identify most insects you find to the level of order. That is, you will be able to tell a beetle (Coleoptera) from a bug (Hemiptera), and a bug (Hemiptera) from an aphid (Homoptera). Sometimes it is important to be able to identify an insect more exactly, but often, figuring out what order an insect belongs to will be enough to help you make sense of your observations and find reference materials to further your work.

Field guides

Field guides are books designed to help people recognize the plants, animals, and minerals that surround us. Many have been written about insects. They have drawings or photographs of insects that you can compare to the actual animal you are looking at, and written descriptions to check. Look for a field guide to the insects native to your area at your local library or bookstore.

But what kind of beetle is it?

If you find an insect and want to figure out exactly what kind it is, you may have quite a challenge ahead of you. For one thing, there are so many species of insects that it is impossible to become familiar with all—or even most—of them. For another, sometimes different species resemble one another quite closely. Many insects are small, and you

may need a hand lens or microscope to find the tiny anatomical features that distinguish them. To complicate matters further, some insects go through dramatic changes during their lives. An insect may look entirely different as a larva than it does as an adult. A male may be different colors than a female of the same species. It takes experience and careful study to make accurate identifications, so call on a local county agent, teacher, naturalist, museum curator, or professional entomologist if you get stuck.

Fortunately, identifying insects is not always difficult. In some cases it is easy to know a species because of distinguishing characteristics that are easy to see. For example, the red bands and spots on the wings of the cecropia moth, *Hyalophora cecropia,* set it apart from the polyphemus moth, *Antheraea polyphemus,* a similar looking species in the same family. Sometimes behavior is a clue to a species identification; a white butterfly flitting around the broccoli or cabbage plants in a garden is bound to be *Pieris rapae,* the cabbage butterfly.

103

Meet the Arthropods

Even if you've never heard of an arthropod before, you already know plenty of them. Spiders, beetles, grasshoppers, crabs, and centipedes are all arthropods, as are centipedes, butterflies, lobsters, and houseflies. In fact, almost three-quarters of all the species of animals in the world belong to the huge **phylum** of Arthropoda, and arthropods live in almost every environment on our planet, from the Arctic Ocean to your own backyard and basement.

What is it that makes all these very different animals part of the same phylum? The word "arthropod" comes from the Greek phrase "jointed foot," and jointed legs are one thing that almost all arthropods have. Most of them also have a tough outer skin called an exoskeleton, which protects them and gives their bodies a solid shape. In addition, many arthropods also have bodies that are made up out of smaller sections, called segments. You can't always see the segments, and some arthropods don't have clear segments, but they are a very common feature of the arthropod body plan.

Arthropods do some amazing things, like molting, when they outgrow and shed their old exoskeleton for a new one. Even watching them move and eat can be fascinating. But you need to be able to watch them for a long time to see these things, and they normally don't like to get too close to people. For that reason, many of the field trips and projects in this chapter are designed to help you collect and study your own specimens. You'll set up a temporary home for a praying mantis (p. 110), and witness the amazing metamorphosis of a caterpillar into a monarch butterfly (p. 112). And in the water, you'll be able to fish for crabs (p. 118) and learn how crayfish defend their territory (p. 122). As before, most of the specimens and equipment are available from the supply houses listed on page 124.

Who's Who Among the Arthropods

Over one million different kinds of animals are known to live on our planet, and about three-quarters of them are arthropods! Scientists divide the animals in the phylum Arthropoda into nine or ten classes. This book will help you get acquainted with six of those classes.

Characteristics of some arthropod classes

THE CENTIPEDES — CLASS CHILOPODA

Centipedes have fangs and a poisonous bite, and most are active predators. Adults have 15–20 pairs of legs, with one pair growing from each body segment. Centipedes have one pair of antennae, three pairs of jaws, and **simple eyes** that don't form images. Their bodies are covered with a smooth, flexible material.

THE MILLIPEDES — CLASS DIPLOPODA

Most millipedes have long, worm-like bodies covered with a tough exoskeleton, but a few are soft-bodied. Adults have between 13 and 100 pairs of legs, depending on the species. Two pairs of legs grow from each **body ring** (each ring is made up of two segments). Millipedes have one pair of antennae on their heads and one pair of jaws. Most millipedes are scavengers.

CRUSTACEANS — CLASS CRUSTACEA

Most crustaceans live in water, but a few, like the pillbugs, live on land. Some crustaceans breathe through gills, but others get oxygen directly through the surface of their bodies.

Many crustaceans use both gills and body surfaces to breathe. Most crustaceans have two pair of antennae in front of their mouths and at least three pairs of jaws. Lobsters, crabs, shrimp, pillbugs, and barnacles are all crustaceans.

THE INSECTS — CLASS INSECTA

An insect's body has three major parts: a head, a middle section called the **thorax**, and an abdomen. (It is not always easy to distinguish these parts.) A pair of antennae grow on the head, and three pairs of legs grow from the thorax. Many adult insects have wings, and most have large **compound eyes** in addition to simple eyes. Beetles, flies, and cicadas are all insects.

SPIDERS AND THEIR RELATIVES — CLASS ARACHNIDA

Arachnids have two main body parts: a **fused** or joined head and thorax, called the **cephalothorax**, and an abdomen. Most have four pairs of legs and simple eyes. They do not have antennae. Some arachnids breathe through special organs called **book lungs**, while others get oxygen directly through their body surfaces or through special tubes. Most arachnids prey on other arthropods, but only a few can chew solid food. The rest pour digestive enzymes onto their prey and then suck up the liquid that results.

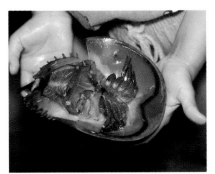

HORSESHOE CRABS — CLASS MEROSTOMATA

Horseshoe crabs have a flattened, horseshoe-shaped cephalothorax and an abdomen that ends in a long, spine-like tail. They have both compound and simple eyes. They also have five pairs of walking legs. In young crabs and in females, the first pair of walking legs end in pincers. In males they look more like boxing gloves or mittens. There are only five living species of horseshoe crabs.

Classification

There are different ways to **classify**, or group, the thousands of kinds of arthropods that live on our planet. Sometimes it is useful to group together those that live in a particular place, or those that have a certain way of moving or feeding. (For instance, lice, ticks, many mites, and some wasps are **parasites**; they live in or on the bodies of other living animals. Most millipedes, however, are **scavengers**; they eat dead plants.) Other times, it is helpful to group animals based on the way their bodies look and work, and on their evo-

Taxonomy

PHYLUM: **Arthropoda** (animals with paired, jointed legs and a hard exoskeleton)
CLASS: **Insecta** (the insects)
ORDER: **Orthoptera** (crickets, grasshoppers, and their relatives)
GENUS: **Dissosteira**
SPECIES: **Dissosteira carolina** (carolina grasshopper)

lutionary history. Scientists pay particular attention to body plan and evolutionary history in deciding which animals to group together in the phylum Arthropoda.

Any phylum can be further divided. Scientists sort the animals in a phylum into **classes**, then divide each class into **orders**. Each order is again divided into families, and families are further divided into **genera**. Each time a division is made, the animals that are most closely related are grouped together. Finally, animals are sorted into distinct **species**, or kinds, and each species is assigned a special, two-part Latin name. Classifying animals is called **taxonomy**. If you are interested in the way scientists classify the animals in this book, look for the Taxonomy boxes on different pages, such as this one for the carolina grasshopper.

IN THE GARDEN

Flower and vegetable gardens are good places to find spiders, insects, and other arthropods. If you don't have a garden yourself, visit a neighbor's garden, or go to a local farm, park, or community garden. You will have the best luck finding arthropods in gardens that are not sprayed with pesticides, so make sure to ask about this. You'll also be taking care of yourself, because pesticides can be harmful to humans as well as to weeds and bugs.

Where to look

Some arthropods will be easy to find. You may see bees flying from flower to flower, or grasshoppers leaping out of your way as you walk along the garden path. You will have to look more closely to find others. Some arthropods cling to plant stems or the undersides of leaves. Still others may be the same color as the plants they are on, making them difficult to spot.

Arthropods make changes in a garden. They often leave traces that tell you where they've been and what they've been doing, such as:
- holes nibbled in leaves or vegetables
- squiggly pathways or tunnels that have been "mined" in leaves
- eggs, empty eggshells, or cocoons
- spider webs

Try looking for arthropods:
- on and under garden mulch
- on and under leaves
- along stems
- in and on flowers
- on the ground

The holes in the leaves of this broccoli plant were probably nibbled by a green caterpillar, the larva of the cabbage white butterfly.

Garden Beetles

Asparagus beetles live in the eastern United States. Look for them on asparagus plants, their sole source of food. Adult beetles are small, but their bright colors make them stand out. Common asparagus beetles have dark wings with yellowish spots, and spotted asparagus beetles are red with black spots. You'll have to look hard to find the larvae, whose dark blue-green bodies match the asparagus almost perfectly.

Most gardeners like having ladybugs around, because they eat aphids and other small, soft-bodied insects that can damage plants. Even though most people call them "bugs," scientists group these insects with the Coleoptera, or beetles, because they have a hard, shiny covering over their wings, and chewing mouthparts. There are about 400 different species of ladybugs in North America; many are orange or yellow with black spots.

Praying Mantids

Praying mantids live in fields, gardens, vacant lots, and other open place where they can find plants to climb on and insects to eat. Depending on the species, a full-grown mantis may be anywhere from two to five inches long. Even so, you may have to look hard to find one. Mantids are green or light brown and tend to blend in with the plants they walk among.

This mantis may keep perfectly still, but will strike if another insect comes near enough.

Mantis life

Young mantids, called **nymphs**, hatch from eggs. Nymphs look like small versions of their parents, except that they lack wings. From the start they are hunters, and will eat any insects they are able to catch. A mantis stands extremely still when it hunts, holding its front legs up as if praying. It seems to be doing nothing, but actually it is keeping a sharp look-out for insects. If one happens to wander near, the mantis shoots out its spiny forelegs, both grabbing and stabbing its prey. Mantis nymphs go through several molts before reaching their full size. As they grow, they are able to handle larger and larger insects. There have even been reports of mantids grabbing toads, shrews, and small birds!

Mantis love

In cool climates, mantids mate during the summer and early fall. Afterwards, the females lay between 40 and 500 eggs in a frothy substance that hardens into a protective egg case. Though the females die when cold weather hits, their eggs can withstand the winter. Male mantids may not even live to see the winter, for they are often devoured by their mates while mating, or just after. This is a gruesome practice from a human standpoint, but scientists think it may actually serve an important purpose for mantids. It could be that females who get a large, protein-rich meal—such as a male mantid—during or just after mating are able to lay more eggs than they otherwise could. If so, a mated pair that "sacrifices" the male may have a better chance of producing young.

Mantis egg case

Native or import

Many of our most familiar mantids are actually **introduced species**. That is, they did not originally live here, but eggs or adults were imported by people. For instance, the European mantis was accidentally sent from Europe to New York State on plants that were shipped to a nursery in 1899. This species now ranges throughout the northeast and into Canada. The Carolina mantis, on the other hand, is a **native species**. It can be found in many southeastern states. Introduced species are often considered pests, but many people appreciate the European and Chinese mantids because they eat other insects that are even more pesty.

Raising mantids

Mantids are fascinating to watch, and easy to raise if you keep their needs and habits in mind.

Housing: An old fish tank or a gallon glass jar makes a good mantis cage. Make a lid out of window screen or mosquito netting. Put a little dirt in the bottom of the cage and add a clump of weeds or grass to give your mantis something to climb on. You can spray a little water on the weeds and soil from time to time, but take care not to create a soggy, humid environment in the cage.

Numbers: Mantids are solitary animals, so keep only one in each cage.

Taxonomy

CLASS: **Insects**

ORDER: **Some scientists group mantids with the Orthoptera (crickets, grasshoppers, and roaches), some group them with the roaches in the order Dictyoptera, and others put them in a separate order altogether, called Mantodea.**
There are 20 species of mantids in North America, including:
- **European mantis, Mantis religiosa**
- **Carolina mantis, Phasmomantis carolina**

You can make a temporary home for a mantid from an old fish tank or a simple gallon jar.

If you crowd them, they are likely to eat one another.

Food and Water: Keep your mantid supplied with live insects to eat. Catch insects outside or buy live crickets at a pet store that sells them for lizard food.

Hatching your own: If you find a mantis egg case that has not yet hatched, you may want to bring it home and keep it until it does. Carry it home, plant stem and all, since trying to remove it from the stem might damage it. If you live where winters are cool, keep the egg case in your refrigerator so it does not hatch right away. Otherwise you'll be overrun with baby mantids at a time of year when it is almost impossible to find food for them! In late spring, when the weather is warm and you are finding lots of insects outdoors, move the egg case out of the refrigerator and into a jar with a screen lid. When the new mantids emerge, keep a few to raise and let the rest go. Newly hatched mantids are tiny, and they will need tiny food. Try miniature prey, like aphids and fruit flies. As they grow, you can add larger insects to their diet.

Mail-order mantids: If you can't listed on page 124. Check to see if you can get one from a species that lives wild in your area. If you can't, you'll need to make sure you don't let your hatchlings loose outdoors.

Raising a Monarch

he monarch, *Danaeus plexippus*, is a large, slow-flying, black and orange butterfly. It is easy to raise a monarch butterfly from an egg or caterpillar that you find outside. If you live in the southern United States, start looking for them in March or April. Further north, you probably won't spot any until May, June, or even later.

Find some milkweed

If you want to find a monarch egg or caterpillar, you will first need to find some milkweed. Monarch caterpillars are picky eaters—they will only eat leaves of the common milkweed, *Ascelpias syriaca,* and its close relatives. A female monarch butterfly cements each of her eggs to the underside of a milkweed leaf so that each new caterpillar hatches right on its food.

Look for milkweed in fields, vacant lots, and along roadsides. In the spring you can recognize the common milkweed by the furry undersides of its oblong leaves and by the sticky white sap that oozes out if you pick a leaf or tear it. In the summer, you'll also notice large clusters of pink flowers. Once you have found a milkweed plant, check the underside of each leaf. If you find a tiny egg or a striped caterpillar, take it home. Don't try to remove the egg from the leaf. Simply cut the stem of the milkweed with a knife or scissors, then carry the plant home with the egg still in place.

Housing and care

An old fish tank, a gallon glass jar, or a cage made from a piece of wire screening and two round cake pans will make a fine temporary home for your monarch. You can even use a cardboard box with a screen or plastic wrap window taped on one side. If your container is glass or smooth plastic, drape a piece of cheesecloth or netting along one side to give your caterpillar—and eventually your butterfly—something to cling to. Cheesecloth or netting can also be used to make a lid. Just cut out a piece a little larger than the opening of your container and fasten it on with a rubber band.

You will need to keep your caterpillar supplied with fresh milkweed to eat. Place a milkweed stalk in a small jar of water and cover the opening with foil or plastic so that your caterpillar does not fall in and drown. Replace the milkweed whenever the leaves begin to look dry or shriveled, or when your caterpillar has eaten most of them. Try to get young, tender leaves, since they are the easiest to chew.

A large caterpillar will eat lots of leaves, and produce plenty of waste, or **frass**. When its cage needs cleaning, simply wipe the frass out with a tissue or paper towel.

Things to look for

You can expect a monarch egg to hatch within four days. The tiny caterpillar that emerges will eat its eggshell, and then will start eating the milkweed. Soon it will molt and grow.

Over the next ten days or so, the caterpillar will go through several more cycles of eating, molting, and growing. Long black antennae will develop on its head, and shorter, antenna-like stalks will grow near its rear end. When the caterpillar eats, you may be able to get a good look at its legs and mouthparts, and see how it uses them. Keep track of how much milkweed you put in the cage, and try to figure out how much your caterpillar eats in a day.

When the caterpillar is about 10–14 days old, it will stop eating. It may seem sick, but actually, it is preparing for a special molt. You may see it spin a small web of silk under a milkweed leaf or on the top of the cage. Or you may notice that it is hanging upside-down from the web with its body curved like the letter **J**. Keep an eye on it at this point, so you can watch the amazing change that happens next.

The upside-down caterpillar will start to wriggle. Finally, its skin will split open and you will see that a **chrysalis** has formed underneath it. At first, the chrysalis will look bright green, but over the next 9–15 days it will turn clear. As it changes, you will be able to see the wings of the butterfly that is developing inside.

Finally, the chrysalis will split open and a damp, crumpled butterfly will crawl out. Over the next hour or two, you can watch it pump fluid into its wings. When the wings look firm and dry, the monarch is ready to fly and you can let it go.

113

Plant a Garden for Butterflies

 f you want to attract butterflies to your home or school, plant a garden for them. Choose plants that provide adult butterflies with **nectar** to drink, and caterpillars with the proper leaves to chew on.

Plan before you plant

Before you actually plant your garden, try to find out what kinds of butterflies live near you, and what plants they use for food. Spend some time outside looking for butterflies and caterpillars, and keep track of the plants they visit. If you don't know the names of the butterflies and plants you see, describe and sketch them in a notebook. Later, you can compare your notes with the descriptions in a field guide, or show them to a knowledgeable gardener or insect-lover. Once you know that a particular plant attracts butterflies, you can put it on the list of possible species to plant in your garden.

Plant a bit of baby food

Though an adult butterfly will drink nectar from many different flowers, its larvae, or caterpillars, usually need a particular type of leaf to eat. Monarch larvae, for example, feed on milkweed, while black swallowtail caterpillars eat carrots, parsley, and Queen Anne's lace. If you want butterflies to lay their eggs in your garden as well as sip nectar there, plant some flowers, shrubs or vegetables that provide food for their young. Field guides, butterfly books, and your own observations will help you figure out which food plants to try out in your garden.

Go native

Gardeners often grow **cultivated** plants. These have been developed by plant breeders to produce many large vegetables or showy blossoms. Gardeners also tend to plant species that did not originally live in the area where they garden. A New England garden may include poppies that grow wild in California or China, irises from Siberia, and cosmos from Mexico. But people who care about butterflies and other arthropods

This tiger swallowtail butterfly will lay its eggs on the leaves of birch, cherry, or ash trees.

believe that it's important to plant many native species in a garden. This is because the plants and animals that naturally **evolved** together in a particular region depend on one another. Monarch butterflies *need* milkweed—without it they cannot produce a new generation of butterflies. And milkweed, in turn, depends on the monarch and many other insects to pollinate it. When we change natural areas to make room for roads and lawns, we eliminate places where butterflies can find food and lay eggs. Replanting native species in areas where they have been destroyed can help butterflies survive.

Planting and tending

If you already have a garden at home or school, you can convert it into a butterfly garden by adding some new plants. If you are starting from scratch, choose a sunny spot that is protected from strong winds. Prepare the soil by removing grass and weeds, and loosening it with a

Bee balm, Monarda didyma, *is visited by hummingbirds as well as butterflies. It is native from New York to Minnesota and south.*

Various species of goldenrod, Solidago spp., *grow in different parts of North America. Goldenrod is an important food source for butterflies during the late summer and early fall, when most other flowers have* **gone to seed**.

garden fork or spade. If the soil is poor, you can add peat moss or rotted manure. Once the soil is ready, add your plants. Spread leaf litter or rotted compost around the base of your plants, to shelter larvae and **pupae**. And keep your garden pesticide-free! Weed and insect killers can be unhealthy for you, and may kill the animals you are trying to attract and observe.

If you don't have room for a garden

Plant a few flowers, herbs, or vegetables that attract butterflies in a large pot or window box. Or see if there is a community garden in your neighborhood that you can share. If you can't find a place to make a garden, then find a place to visit one. Many communities have botanical gardens, parks, and other areas that are planted with flowers.

Queen Anne's lace, Daucus carota, *or wild carrot, was brought to America by colonists and now grows wild in many places. It is a food plant for black swallowtail caterpillars.*

More than 100 species of milkweed grow naturally in North America. The beautiful butterfly weed, Asclepias tuberosa, *is a favorite with gardeners.*

Finding native plants

It is tempting to dig up wildflowers wherever you find them, but this is not the best way to acquire plants for your garden! You might unknowingly take plants that are rare, or transplant flowers that will not thrive in their new home. Instead, buy native plants at a nursery, or start your own from seeds. If you call or write to them, the National Wildflower Research Center (2600 FM 973 North, Austin TX 78725, (512) 929-3600) can help you figure out what to plant in your area. For $3.50, you can also buy a guide to native plants from The Soil Conservation Society of America (7515 NE. Ankeny Road, Ankeny IA 50021, (515) 289–2331). And if you want to find the botanical club or native plant society nearest to you, contact the New England Wildflower Society at the Garden in the Woods, Hemenway Road, Framingham, MA 01701, (508) 877-7630).

AT THE GROCERY STORE

You may not have thought of looking for arthropods at the grocery store, but a grocery store with a good seafood department is one of the best places to get a look at a live lobster. In fact, you are far more likely to see a live lobster at the store than at the shore, because lobsters stay under the water and tend to move around at night. Fish markets, restaurants, and aquariums are also good places to look for lobsters. There are about 135 different kinds of lobsters in the world's oceans. The species sold in most North American markets is the northern lobster, *Homarus americanus*.

Lobster anatomy

When lots of lobsters are crowded together in a tank, it can be hard to see them clearly. Ask the person in charge of the tank if he or she will take one out for you to study. A grocery store lobster usually has a band around each of its two large claws, or chelipeds, so you can handle it without getting pinched. Wild lobsters use these claws to protect themselves and to catch prey. You'll notice that one claw is longer and more slender than the other. This claw, sometimes called the "ripper" or "pincher" claw, is lined with sharp teeth. It is used to grab prey and tear it apart. The short, wide claw is lined with bumps called tubercules, and is adapted for crushing.

You'll notice that your lobster has a hard shell covering its midsection, or thorax. If you turn it over, you can see that the legs that hold the large front claws are attached to the underside of the thorax. Four other pairs of jointed legs follow the large-clawed pair. They are used for walking, and the first two pair, which end in pincers, are also used to catch food. From underneath, you may also

be able to see the lobster's mouthparts, which are on its head, just in front of the first pair of legs.

A lobster's abdomen is divided into segments and ends in a tail fan, called the telson. Joints between each segment make the abdomen flexible. A lobster can even snap its telson under it and shoot backwards through the water. Small paddle-like swimmerets on the underside of some of the segments help the lobster swim forward. If you want to find out whether your lobster is male or female, check the pair of small appendages that grow from the underside of the first abdominal segment. In a female, they will be small and rather soft. In a male, they are hard and bony. The male's appendages transfer sperm to the female during mating. The telson can also help you determine the sex of your lobster: it is broader in females than in males.

Here is a northern lobster, showing the underside and back. Notice the five pairs of legs on the thorax, the mouthparts in front of them, and the small swimmerets along the abdomen.

Lobsters depend on their two sets of antennae for information about their environment.

How a lobster knows the world

A lobster's eyes probably don't see images, as human eyes do. In the dim light under sea, they work more like motion detectors. In the bright light of a grocery store or kitchen, they are useless. A lobster knows the world through touch and "smell." Like other crustaceans, a lobster has two pairs of antennae on its head. The long antennae are sensitive "feelers." The short pair detect chemicals, acting something like an underwater nose. Tiny hairs on the lobster's legs and feet also help it feel and "smell."

Growing up

The lobsters you see in the store may be five years old or even older. Each started out as a tiny egg no larger than the head of a pin. It was carried around on its mother's tail and swimmerets for 9–11 months until it hatched. A newly hatched lobster looks very different from the adults you see in the store. It has no claws, and instead of crawling on the ocean bottom, it floats near the surface of the water. After a few molts, it develops claws. By the fourth molt it is a little less than an inch long and looks like its older relatives. Lobsters can grow to be very large and very old. Some have reached lengths of 24, or even 34 inches and weighed in at 30–44 pounds. No one is sure how old these really big lobsters are, but some scientists think the oldest ones might be close to 100 years old!

Taxonomy

CLASS: *Crustacea*
ORDER: *Decapoda (decapods, including crabs, shrimp, lobsters and crayfish, all have ten legs)*
FAMILIES: *Homaridae or Nephrosidae (true lobsters)*
Palinuridae (spiny lobsters)
Scylliridae (slipper or Spanish lobsters)
Polychelidae (deep-sea lobsters)
GENUS AND SPECIES: *Homarus americanus*

In the wild

In the wild, northern lobsters are solitary animals. During the day they take shelter in crevices and burrows. At night they come out to look for food. They will eat live clams, starfish, and other prey, munch on algae and eelgrass, and scavenge dead animals from the ocean floor. Lobsters are territorial and will try to keep other lobsters away from their burrows. A large lobster will even eat a smaller one that strays too close. Bait stolen from lobster traps can also be an important part of a lobster's diet.

Many marine animals prey on young lobsters. Though a female can produce 10,000 or 20,000 eggs at a time, only 10–20 of the young that hatch will survive more than a month. Large lobsters have few predators other than people.

This is a drawing of the first larval stage of a lobster, right after it hatches. It is only one-third of an inch long.

FISHING FOR CRABS

Next time you go to the beach, plan to spend part of your time fishing. Some people like to catch bluefish, striped bass, and other good-tasting ocean fish, but if you are interested in arthropods, try fishing for crabs instead. You probably won't want to eat your catch, but you're bound to have fun watching it.

Things you'll need
- old sneakers or water shoes to protect your feet
- several long pieces of string
- a chicken wing for bait
- a plastic bucket

Directions
1. Find a safe, comfortable place to sit or stand.
2. Choose a piece of string long enough to reach down to the water from where you plan to fish. Then tie the chicken wing securely to one end of it.
3. Dangle the chicken wing in the water and wait for a while.
4. You may not feel it when a crab grabs onto the wing, so pull your bait up from time to time and take a look. Pull the wing up slowly, so that any hangers-on don't get washed off.
5. If there is a crab on your line, gently pull it off and put it in your bucket. Take care to keep your fingers away from its pinching claws! Or simply lower the crab, chicken wing and all, into your bucket for viewing.
6. When you are done observing your crab, let it go where you found it.
7. You can store your string and bait in the freezer for another day, or just throw them away.

Where to fish?
You can try fishing for crabs from a dock or from the water's edge. Choose a spot where the water is shallow and relatively calm. This is important for your own safety, as well as for your fishing success. If the waves are rough and the water

deep, any crabs you catch are likely to be knocked back into the water when you try to pull them out. More importantly, you might get swept into the water yourself. An adult should help you find a safe spot. Of course, you need to pick a spot where crabs live. If you don't know of one already, try fishing in tide pools and around rocks and clumps of seaweed, where the water is shallow and crabs can find shelter.

Nets and traps

In shallow water, you can scoop up crabs with a net. You can also collect crabs in special traps that look like cages. Put a bit of chicken or some other bait in the trap, then lower it into the water. Pull it up later to see if any crabs have found their way into it.

Substitute bait

Many crabs are scavengers, eating dead animals and whatever else they find lying around. They use their large pinching claws to pick up bits of food and pass it to their mouths. Crabs can see, but their ability to detect chemicals in the water is probably more important to them when it comes to finding food. A crab that finds your chicken wing has "smelled" or "tasted" it underwater. If you don't happen to have a chicken wing on hand, you can try catching crabs with another kind of bait— perhaps a bit of hot dog or a piece of ham from a sandwich. Just be aware that these foods are more difficult to secure to a fishing line.

Woodlice

oodlice, the sowbugs, pillbugs, and roly-poly bugs, are crustaceans. Unlike most of their crustacean relatives, however, woodlice live on land. Look for them in leaf litter, gardens, woodpiles, under logs and stones, and in other damp places.

What woodlice are like

Most woodlice are small, flat, and gray. Like other crustaceans, they have two pairs of antennae on their heads. The first pair is so tiny that you may not even notice it, but the second pair is easy to see. A woodlouse has seven body segments just behind its small head; these make up its thorax, or mid-section. Each segment has a pair of legs growing from it. The thorax is followed by the abdomen, which has six narrow segments. The last segment has two "tails," called **uropods**, growing from it. Pillbugs have short, inconspicuous uropods, but the ones on sowbugs are quite noticeable. Woodlice also have appendages called **pleopods** growing from the rest of their abdominal segments. Some of these are used as gills, to get oxygen from the air. Woodlice are scavengers—they eat decaying plants, fungi, and bits of organic material in the soil.

Family life

When woodlice mate, the male transfers sperm into the female's body with his second pair of pleopods. When the female is ready to lay her eggs, she deposits them in a special **brood pouch** on the underside of her thorax. She continues to carry her young in her brood pouch once they hatch, taking them wherever she goes. After about three weeks, the young are able to live on their own.

After a rain, or early in the morning when the air is still damp, you might spot a woodlouse crawling on a tree trunk.

Perhaps some woodlice have been nibbling on this mushroom.

A mother pillbug with her young.

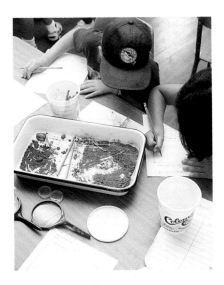

Raising woodlice

You can keep woodlice in a terrarium. Add some well-decayed leaf litter, bark, or bits of moss to provide them with food. Keep the soil moist, but not damp or soggy. At times, you may want to take a few woodlice out and put them in a small dish or pan so that you can observe them more easily. Just remember that they need a humid environment in order to survive, and limit the amount of time you keep them out in the dry air.

Sowbug or pillbug?

When you first start looking at woodlice, they may all look the same to you. But if you study them closely, you can learn to tell different kinds apart. Two groups that you are likely to find are the sowbugs and the pillbugs. Sowbugs have flat, oval bodies and two distinct uropods. A pillbug's body, on the other hand, is more curved, or arched, on the top and its uropods are so short that you may not even notice them. When a pillbug is disturbed, it will roll up into a ball. A few species of sowbugs can do this as well, but most cannot.

121

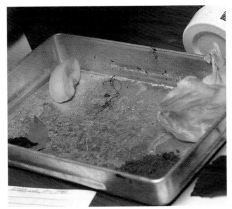

Create different conditions within a small pan by arranging different kinds of soil, stones, and leaves inside. Add a few woodlice and watch to see where they go. Do they prefer to be on or under things? On soil, stones, or leaves? What will woodlice eat? Test out some different possibilities.

Crayfish

rayfish are common in rivers, lakes, ponds and streams. Some species climb around on land at night, returning to burrows in damp soil when they are through foraging for food. Many kinds of crayfish are easy to raise and interesting to watch. Collect some from a local pond or order a few live ones from a supply company (see page 62).

Housing

Keep crayfish in an aquarium or a plastic tub with a layer of clean gravel on the bottom. Some species do best in very shallow water that doesn't quite cover their bodies. Others need deeper water and a filter and aerator for their tank. If you collect your own crayfish, pay careful attention to the water level where you find them and try to duplicate it at home. Mail-order crayfish will arrive with care instructions. Most crayfish do best in clean, well-oxygenated water, so change the water daily if you are not filtering it. Tap water is usually fine for crayfish.

Put a few rocks in the tank so that your crayfish can climb out of the water from time to time. Rock piles or clean clay flower pots will provide burrows for them to hide in. If the tank is large with several hiding places, you can try keeping several crayfish in it. But keep an eye out for fighting and other aggressive behavior; these are signs that you need a bigger tank or fewer crayfish.

Feeding

Crayfish are scavengers and will eat all sorts of food. You can offer them bits of raw fish, meat, dog or cat food, and aquatic plants. Put the food right in front of them and if they don't start eating it within five minutes or so, remove it and try again later. Feed your crayfish three times a week, and change the water after each feeding. If you want, you can move each one to a small pan or dish for feeding so that it's easier to keep the tank water clean.

Here are two different kinds of tanks you can set up for crayfish. The shallow one (above) is better for species that live in shallow water and like to come out on rocks occasionally. The tank on the right is deeper, and has an aerator. If you don't use an aerator, make sure to change the tank water every day.

Observe your crayfish while you feed them, and make note of what they like to eat.

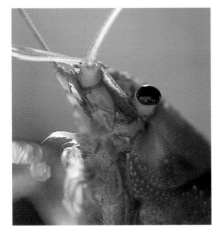

Crayfish anatomy

Pick up a crayfish and get familiar with the way it looks. You'll notice that it has a hard shell, or **carapace**, covering its fused head and thorax. On the head, look for:

- two large compound eyes on movable stalks
- two pairs of antennae. Both pairs are important sensory organs. The first pair, called the antennules, are shorter than the second, and contain organs that help the crayfish keep its balance.
- five pairs of jointed appendages that serve as mouthparts. One pair is also used to clean the antennae, and another moves water across the gills, which are underneath the carapace.

On the thorax, look for five pairs of walking legs. The first pair end in large claws which the crayfish uses

to crush its food and to defend itself. Some of the crayfish you find might not have all ten of their legs. If a crayfish's leg is grabbed by a predator, or in a fight with another crayfish, it often breaks off. A tiny new leg will appear after the next molt and grow larger as time goes by.

Crayfish have swimmerets on the underside of their abdomens. In adult males, as in adult male lobsters, the first pair look different from the rest. These two swimmerets are long and hard and are used to transfer sperm to the female. Female crayfish tend to have wider abdomens than males, and smaller front claws.

Behavior

Watch how your crayfish use the various parts of their bodies and how they interact with each other. If you have a few crayfish and want to make sure you can tell them apart, give each one a distinctive mark with nail polish. Dry off the carapace with a paper towel so that the nail polish will stick. Over time, try to find out:

Notice the five pairs of walking legs and the swimmerets behind.

Taxonomy

CLASS: *Crustacea*
ORDER: *Decapoda*
FAMILIES: *Astacidae,
    Cambarinae
    (500 species worldwide)
    Procambarus blandingi,
    the species in most of
    these photos, is common
    in pools and slow
    moving streams.*

Mark your crayfish so you can study their individual behavior.

- Whether your crayfish are able to swim.
- When your crayfish are most active. Observe them at different times of the day and night, on cloudy and sunny days, and with the room lights on and off.
- What a crayfish does when you approach it, or when another crayfish comes near.
- Whether particular crayfish "hang out" in specific parts of the tank.
- If the crayfish in your tank seem to get along as equals, or if one **dominates** the others by displaying aggressive behavior until they retreat.

123

How to Order Specimens and Equipment

Carolina Biological
Supply
2700 York Road
Burlington, NC 27215
Toll free: 1-800-334-5551

The most interesting way to study animals and plants is to go out and collect as many specimens as you can. And it's easy to make your own equipment by adapting old pans, bowls, and other kitchen and hobby supplies. Sometimes though, depending on the season and where you live, it can be hard to find live specimens, and some kinds of equipment, like microscopes, can't be made at home.

Almost all the specimens and equipment can be ordered through the mail or over the phone from a company called Carolina Biological Supply. If you want to order by phone, you'll need an adult with a credit card. A handling charge will be added to each order.

Please remember: If you order live specimens, make sure you have everything you need to feed and house them before they arrive. If the specimens are not native to your part of the country, it is very important that you not let them into the wild after studying them—letting them loose in a new environment could disturb the ecological balance in your area. If you're not sure, ask the people at Carolina Biological Supply. If you do have to kill a specimen, freezing it is probably the safest and least painful method. Also, please keep in mind that the prices and other information for the items below are subject to change.

Adventures in Woods, Ponds, and Fields

Earthworms (p. 14)
12 medium-sized live earthworms, #L408, $5.99
Magic Worm Food, 12-oz. bag, #L399A, $2.50

Snails (p. 16)
12 live land snails, #L480, $7.98

Using a Berlese Funnel (p. 20)
Berlese Funnel Set, #65-4148, $13.50

Summer Singers (p. 24)
12 adult house crickets, #L715, $4.95
"Little Chirper" Cricket Cage (with six crickets), #L717, $11.50

Collecting and Pressing Plants (p. 26)
Leaf and Flower Press (with 15 layers of blotting paper, #66-3045, $13.10

Microinvertebrates (p. 30)
Panasonic Light Scope 30x pocket microscope, #59-4900, $34.95

Investigations with Planaria (p. 36)
15 mature live planaria, #L210, $4.80
Planaria heads and tails kit, for studying regeneration, #L237, $21.55

Exploring the World of Birds

Getting Started (p. 40)
Wolfe Economy 8 x 30 Prism Binoculars, #60-2560, $79.95

Identifying Birds (p. 42)
Field Guides: Your local bookstore should have a selection of field guides to birds in your area, but here are some that Carolina Biological Supply sells:
Birds (Golden Guides), #45-5080, $3.95
Audubon Field Guide to Eastern Birds, #45-5096, or Western Birds, #45-5096A, each $15.95.
Stokes Guide to Bird Behavior (Vol. 1), #45-5073, $9.95
Peterson's Guide to Bird Nests, #45-5072A, $13.95

What Owls Eat (p. 48)
Owl Pellets, #P1680, $3.20 each or 12 for $32.00

Hatching Chicks (p. 50)
Incubator, #70-1191, $41.00
Curtained Brooder, #70-1225, $29.00

Fertile Chicken Eggs, #L1726,
$15.00 per dozen

Bird Songs and Calls (p. 54)
*Carolina Biological Supply offers
three different bird calls:*
Hawk , #65-1701, $12.45
Bobwhite, #65-1703, $11.25
Songbird, #65-1706, $5.95

Feeding Birds (p. 56)
*Carolina Biological Supply offers a
large selection of feeders and feeder
accessories. Here are some of them:*
Woodkrafter Bird Feeder Kit,
#65-1802, $10.95
Universal Tubular Feeder, #65-1806,
$25.00
Spill Tray for Universal Feeder,
#65-1838, $16.95
Songbird Feed, #65-1847, $5.45 for
a 5 lb. bag
Suet Cone, #65-1854, $4.45
Squirrel Baffle, #65-1835, $29.00

Living at the Seashore

The Sandy Shore (p. 60)
Slide-Out Pocket Magnifier, 5x,
#60-2115, $6.95

Hermit Crabs (p. 66)
Land Hermit Crab, #L 600, $10.35
for three
Hermit Crab Cakes (food for hermit
crabs), #L600R, $5.45 for a
3-oz. bag.

Clams (p. 68)
Preserved Clams for Dissection:
Long-Necked Clam, #P506C,
$1.80 each
Venus Clam, #P513C, $1.90 each
Dissecting Scalpels, #62-5920,
$0.95 each

Investigations with Sponges (p. 72)
Live Sponges, L54G, $12.30 per
set of 15

Setting Up a Salt Water Aquarium (p. 74)
Basic 10-gallon Aquarium Tank Kit,
#67-0146, $73.75
Forty Fathoms Marinemix (instant
sea water formula), #67-1442,
$3.80 for a package that makes
10 gallons of seawater.

Pressing Seaweed (p. 78)
Leaf and Flower Press (with 15
layers of blotting paper),
#66-3045, $13.10. This will
work fine for seaweed as well.

Bugs, Bugs, Bugs

Getting Started (p. 86)
Pacific Aerial Net, #65-1380, $14.75

Dragonflies and Damselflies (p. 92)
Live Dragonfly Nymphs, #L771,
$14.65 per 12
Live Damselfly Nymphs, #L775,
$14.65 per 12

Raising Milkweed Bugs (p. 94)
Milkweed Bug Culture Kit, L840,
$22.00
Milkweed Bug Food, #L848,
$3.75 per 250-g. unit.

Making a Collection (p. 100)
8-oz. Killing Jar, #65-4052, $3.90 each.
Insect Killing Solution, #65-4064,
$3.95 per 2-oz. container
Insect Mounting Board, #65-4190,
$18.70 per 10 boards
Insect Mounting Pins, sizes 0, 1, 2,
& 3, #65-4302, -4303, -4304,
& -4305, $7.65 per 100
Cardboard Insect Box, #65-4780,
$10.50 each

Identifying Insects (p. 102)
Peterson's Field Guide to Insects of
North America, #45-4505, $13.95

Meet the Arthropods

Praying Mantids (p. 110)
Mantis Eggs, #L738, $10.99 per 3

Woodlice (p. 120)
Terrestrial Isopods, #L624,
$5.75 per 12

Crayfish (p. 122)
Live Crayfish, medium, #L592,
$6.90 per 3

Glossary

abdomen: the last body section of an arthropod, or the "belly" of a mammal.

aestivate: to spend time in an unmoving state during a period of hot or dry weather.

alga (pl., algae): a large group of plants that includes many microscopic species that live on land and in water. (Some scientists do not classify algae as plants, but put them in another kingdom.)

annuli: the yearly growth rings on a bivalve shell.

anterior: at or near the front.

aquatic: living in water.

benchmark: the spot chosen to be the "zero point" on a transect.

beneficial animal: any one of various animals that are helpful to people. They eat our pests, or provide us with food and materials.

bivalve: an animal with a two-part shell, such as clams, oysters, and mussels. Bivalves form a class within the phylum of molluscs.

body ring: a section of a millipede's body, made up of two fused body segments and carrying two pairs of legs.

book gills: the breathing organs of horseshoe crabs. Book gills get oxygen from the water by opening and closing like books do, which allows water to pass over the many page-like folds of the gills.

book lungs: the breathing organs of some arachnids. Like book gills, book lungs extract oxygen from the air by opening and closing like books.

boring sponge: any sponge in the family Clionidea, that drills into mollusc shells or corals as it grows.

brood: to keep fertilized eggs within the body until they hatch.

brooder: a heated box chicks are placed in after they hatch.

bud: a piece of a sponge that breaks off and develops into a new sponge.

carapace: the part of an arthropod's exoskeleton that covers the head and thorax.

carbohydrates: chemical compounds made of carbon, oxygen, and hydrogen. Sugars and starches are carbohydrates.

carnivore: a meat-eater.

castings: soil or sediment swallowed by a worm and excreted at the entrance of its tunnel or burrow.

caudal: relating to the tail of an animal.

cephalothorax: the fused head and thorax of spiders and other arachnids.

cerci: abdominal appendages on some insects that pick up information about the surrounding environment.

cheliped: the claw of a lobster or other member of the order Decapoda.

chrysalis: the pupal stage of a butterfly.

cilia: very small, moving, hair-like structures on some cells.

circuli: growth rings on a bivalve shell.

class: a smaller group of living things in one phylum. Each phylum is divided into classes, and each class is further divided into orders.

classify: in biology, to organize living things into different groups.

clitellum: the light-colored "collar" around the body of an earthworm.

commensualism: a relationship between two organisms that benefits one of them and does no harm to the other.

community: a group of organisms that live together in the same place.

compound eyes: an eye made up of many simple eyes that function together.

compound leaf: Leaves divided into two or more parts, or leaflets.

conifer: the group of trees that grow seed cones, including pine and spruce trees.

deciduous: the group of trees and shrubs that lose their leaves at the end of each growing season

decline: a downward slant; downhill.

diameter, outside & inside: the distances from center of a nest to its inside and outside edges. These distances can sometimes be used to identify the species of bird which made the nest.

distress call: the special sound made by an animal when it is in trouble, and which other birds can recognize.

domestic animal: any of the various animals that are used and raised by people.

dominate: to control or rule over others.

dorsal nerve chord: the nerve chord that runs along the back of animals in the phylum Chordata. In humans, the spinal chord.

dorsal: relating to the "back" of an animal, usually the uppermost surface.

egg tooth: the small bump on a chick's beak that it uses to break open the eggshell when it hatches.

elytra: the hard or leathery first pair of wings on an adult beetle.

embryo: an unhatched or unborn animal in the early stages of development.

evolution: for a species, the process of changing physical form over long periods of time.

exoskeleton: the hard, outside body covering of an arthropod.

family: a group of living things. Each order is divided into families, and each family is further divided into genera.

fertile: able to have children.

field marks: distinctive features that can help you tell one animal from another.

filter feeder: an animal that strains minute organisms or particles of food out from water.

free-living: animals that do not live in or on the bodies of other animals; not a parasite.

fungus (pl., fungi): a mushroom, puffball, mold, yeast, or relative of them. Some scientists consider fungi plants, while others put them in a separate kingdom altogether.

fused: joined together without a seam or joint.

gastropod: any member of the class Gastropoda, which in Greek means a "stomach-foot." Gastropods, such as snails, move by means of a long, muscular "foot" that runs the length of their body.

gemmule: a cell that produces new individuals of its own species.

genus (pl., genera): a smaller grouping of species within one family of living things.

gills: organs capable of extracting oxygen from water.

gonads: reproductive organs, such as testes and ovaries, where eggs and sperm are made.

gone to seed: a plant has "gone to seed" for the season when it no longer has any flowers and has released its seeds.

habitat: an organism's environment, the kind of place it usually lives in.

herbarium: a collection of dried and pressed plants.

herbivore: a plant-eater.

hermaphrodite: an animal that has both male and female reproductive organs.

incline: an upward slant; uphill.

incubate: to keep an egg warm so it can develop and hatch.

introduced species: a species of plant or animal brought by people to a place outside its natural environment.

isolate: in biology, to remove something from its natural environment, usually to study it.

kingdom: a group of living things. Scientists group all living things into several divisions, or kingdoms, including animals, plants, and bacteria.

lateral line: a special sensory system in bony fish that helps them detect motions in the water around them.

mantle: a layer of tissue unique to molluscs that forms their shells (when they have them).

membrane: a thin, soft layer of tissue that covers or lines a cell or organ.

metamorphosis: a physical change of form that some animals undergo as they develop.

mollusc: one of the phyla of the animal kingdom. Snails, clams, octopods, and squid are all molluscs.

molt: the process by which arthropods shed their old exoskeletons and form new, usually larger ones.

mucus: a moist, sticky, or slimy secretion.

nares: the nostril-like openings in a fish's snout.

native species: a species of plant or animal that has evolved where it is found.

nectar: a sweet, nutritious fluid secreted by many plants to attract pollinating insects, such as butterflies.

neuromasts: special cells that form a part of the lateral line system in bony fishes.

notochord: a strong, flexible rod that runs along the back of every animal in the phylum Chordata during some phase of its life.

nymphs: the young of any insect that undergoes gradual metamorphosis.

operculum: the gill cover on a bony fish, or the small, hard plate that covers the opening of a snail's shell.

optic lobe: the part of an animal's brain that helps it to see.

order: a group of living things. Each class is divided in orders, and each order is further divided into families.

overwinter: to survive the cold weather of winter in a dormant state. Some butterflies overwinter as pupae.

ovipositors: in a female animal, the organ that deposits the egg in a specific place.

parasite: an organism that lives in or on other organisms. Parasites typically weaken, and sometimes kill, their hosts.

pellets: packets of fur, bones, seeds, and other indigestible material that birds throw up after feeding.

pest: a species that annoys people, or causes harm to food crops or property.

petiole: the stalk or stem of a leaf.

photosynthesize: to use energy from sunlight to make sugar from water and carbon dioxide, the way plants do.

phylum (pl., phyla): a group of living things. The plant and animal kingdoms are divided into phyla.

pipping: to break open the shell of an egg when hatching.

prehensile: able to grab and hold something.

pupa (pl., pupae): in complete metamorphosis, the stage of development between larva and imago, usually occurring within a cocoon or chrysalis.

pupate: in insects, to change from a larva to a pupa (such as a butterfly's chrysalis or cocoon).

radula: a file-like structure in a gastropod's mouth, used to scrape food.

range map: a special map that shows in what areas a given animal or plant species can be found.

reaggregation: reassembling parts to form a whole. Some sponges can reaggregate after they have been broken up.

regeneration: the process of growing back tissues or structures that have been removed or destroyed. A method of reproduction in some animals.

scales: small, hard plates that are part of the external covering of some fish and reptiles.

scavenger: an organism that eats dead plants and animals, or garbage.

segmented: made up of a number of similar sections, like the segmented bodies of arthropods and worms.

sessile: attached to one spot, unable to move. Most plants and some animals, like barnacles, are sessile.

setae: bristle-like organs on some animals.

silhouette: the outline of an object. Some plants and animals, like birds and trees, can be identified by their silhouettes.

simple eyes: eyes capable only of telling the difference between light and darkness.

siphons, inhalent and exhalent: the two tubes that some invertebrates have through which they pull water into their body (the inhalent siphon) and then push it out again (the exhalent siphon).

social insects: those insect species that live together in groups, or colonies. Each member of a colony works to help the whole group survive.

species: a distinct kind of organism. Similar species are grouped together in a genus. Members of a species can mate and produce more organisms like themselves.

spicules: needle-like structures that form the "skeleton" of some sponges.

spring tides: the extra high (and extra low) tides that occur around the time of the full moon and the new moon.

suet: hard fat from sheep or cattle, often used to feed birds.

swimmerets: the small, paddle-like appendages that grow from the underside of a lobster's tail and help it swim.

taxonomy: the science of classifying organisms by grouping them according to shared uniquely evolving physical characteristics.

telson: the final part of a lobster's tail, also called the tail fan.

tendons: tough, cord-like tissues that connect muscles to bone.

tentacles: long, flexible appendages on many invertebrates, used as sensory organs or to grab food.

terrestrial: living on land.

territorial: having a given area or territory. Animals are called territorial when they "claim" a certain area and try to keep other animals out of it.

test: the shed exoskeleton of a crab or horseshoe crab, or the skeleton of a sea urchin or sand dollar.

thorax: the middle section of an arthropod's body

transect: a measuring line that runs though an area. Transects are used to help study a particular environment.

transverse fission: splitting apart crosswise rather than lengthwise.

tube feet: small, tube-like appendages on echinoderms that are used for feeding, moving, or as sensory organs.

tubercules: the bumps that line a lobster's shorter, "crushing" claw.

umbo: the bump near the hinge on each of a clam's two shells. The umbo is the oldest part of the shell, and you can see how much the clam has grown in its life by comparing the sizes of the umbo and the rest of the shell.

univalve: an animal having a one-piece shell, such as whelks, periwinkles, and snails.

vents: openings on the surface of a sponge that push water out of the sponge's body.

wild animal: an animal that is neither tame nor raised by people.